The Army Of God's Generals
Deliverance Manual On
How To Take Back Land, Property, And People

By

Penny Y. Z. Thompson

Paradise Creek Books
www.paradisecreekbooks.com

Unless otherwise noted, Scripture quotations are from the King James Version, *The Personalized Size Giant Print Holy Bible Reference*. Copyright 1994, Zondervan, Grand Rapids.

Printed in the United States of America

First Publication: October 2011

ISBN # 978-0-9836652-6-7

Cover Artist: Debra K. Gaines

Ordering Information
Special discounts are available on quantity purchases. For details, contact Paradise Creek Books at the web address above.

Foreward

Penny Thompson is a precious sister in the Lord. She has an extensive ministry and experience in deliverance. She also has training in the military…the United States Army, where she served as an Army Officer. I will never forget the day she showed up at my network meeting and introduced herself and told me the Lord had given me to her for her next assignment. Over the last many years as a member of our church, I have watched her love for the Lord and faithfulness touch the lives of many. Her personal prayer and intercession for me and Sonrise Christian Center has been such a blessing.

Penny has a heart to see people freed from their bondages. Many people have been healed physically, as well as she has prayed for them. Penny's faith and love are contagious. As I say, Penny's from heaven!

Her manual on deliverance deals with how to take back land, property, and people for Jesus the Lord. The section on root causes for the need to be delivered are very helpful for those in deliverance ministry. The manual should be helpful to you as you seek to see people freed. She shares personal stories and the stories of others to give you insight into deliverance. Her recommendation to be under authority and to be in authority is so needed and Biblical. God continues to use you, Penny, to see people touched by the Holy Spirit.

Dr. Dan Hammer
Senior Pastor
Sonrise Christian Center

Honor and Thanks

I want to give honor and thanks to the following persons who stood with me to see the vision of this book come to pass. Behind every book there are people who pray and stand with you while you fight a battle to see the book finalized for publishing.

I want to honor my Pastors Dr. Dan and Terry Hammer, Pastors Doug and Faith Martin, Pastor Scott and Leann Smith, and Pastors Ron and Dr. Beverly Willis of Liberty Ministry Fellowship Incorporation, and Ron and Melinda Ritz. Thank you for believing in me when I started the process of drafting and writing this book.

I want to honor those who were my proofreaders: Mr. and Mrs. Scott, Kay Rice, and Mrs. Patricia Burke, who without you I could not complete this process.

I want to honor those who spoke prophetic words over the vision of the book: Dr. Chuck Pierce, President of Global Spheres, Incorporation and President of Glory of Zion International, Dr. Steve List, Apostle/Pastor Steve Mayanja, Uganda, Uganda Christian Outreach Ministries, Dr. Matthew

Thomas, India, Chairman Fellowship of Pentecostal Churches, President Central India Theological Seminary, Pastor/Dr. Oluwasayo (Sayo) Ajiboye, Nigeria/Bellevue, Mission Africa International, and Dr. Beverly Willis of Liberty Ministries Fellowship Incorporation .

I would also like to thank all those who interceded and prayed for me while I wrote the book. Thank you Pastors Dr. Dan and Terry Hammer, Pastors Ron and Dr. Beverly Willis, Pastors Doug and Faith Martin, Pastors Scott and Leann Smith, Mrs. Suzanne Tuiasosopo and family, Mr. Leo and MaryAnn Gaceta, Mrs. Mary Malkus, Mrs. Sue Thomson and Mrs. Anita Young, Mrs. Kari Zevenbergen, Mr. and Mrs. Joseph and Jojo Heimbigner, Apostle Tim and Brenda Taylor of Watchman Ministries International, Mr. Ross Hanby, Mr. and Mrs. Scott and Kay Rice, Monica Alvarez, Mrs. Cristina Peterson and Carollee, Chuck and Tammi Gershaw, and Joe and Holly Ruddock and Family.

I also want to give thanks to Mr. Dave Peterson, Mrs. Rebecca Frost, and Mrs. Carolyn Gard. There are so many to thank, so if I did not recognize you, I want to give thanks to all who stood with me and prayed while I took the time to wait on the Lord to begin to unfold and address ways to liberate and set liberty to the captives.

About the Book Cover and the Artist

I want to give honor to the cover artwork created by Artist Debra K. Gaines, www.HealingRainArts.com. She is a prophetic artist who has been painting for thirty years.

The painting depicts the General of God's Army, the Father, the Son, the Holy Spirit and the fivefold ministry that is involved in building the Kingdom of God.

The black background represents the darkness in this world—souls captured by the enemy. The fire represents the Spirit of God that has come in great power and light, igniting God's Army, to bring Freedom to the Captive!

Table of Contents

Foreward   I
Honor and Thanks   3
About the Book Cover and the Artist   5

Chapter One: Deliverance   9
Deliverance through Spiritual Warfare   9
Deliverance is Real   9
How to Deliver the Land That Was Taken Into   15
     Captivity through Spiritual Warfare
A True Life Scenario   19
How to Deliver Personal Property That Has   23
     Fallen Under a Curse
How Deliverance Works   24
How to Deliver People Who Are Under Attack   32
     and Tormented By the Enemy
Why We Need to Know What to Do in Deliverance   33
How Spiritual Weapons are Used by Deliverance   38
     through Spiritual Warfare

Chapter Two: Two Kingdoms   47
How the Two Kingdoms Work   47
How the Chain of Command Works In Both Kingdoms   49
What the Kingdom of Darkness Looks Like and How   54
     It Functions
What the Kingdom of Light Looks Like and How It   61
     Functions

Chapter Three: Demons in the Bible   65
How the Demons in the Bible Serve the Kingdom   65
    Of Darkness
The Spirits That Fall Under Each Demon As   68
    Identified In the Bible

Chapter Four: Root Causes   73
How Root Causes of the Spirit Operate   73
How Access Doors Are Given to the Spirits   74
The Five Access Doors   75
How fo Combat the Spirits   78
Interview Results with Pastors and Ministers   79
Survey of People Who Have Been Delivered   84
Statistics   89

Chapter Five: Case Scenarios   99
Real Deliverance Cases of People Who Were Delivered   100
Reasons for Their Captivity   104
How to Liberate People from Captivity   107
How to Walk Through Deliverance and Set People Free   109
How to Walk After Deliverance to Maintain Your Freedom   111

Chapter Six: Conclusion   113

Works Cited   115

About the Author   117

Chapter One
Deliverance

Hosea 4:6—"My people are destroyed for lack of knowledge, because thou has rejected knowledge, I will also reject thee, that thou shall be no priest to me, seeing thou hast forgotten thy children."

Deliverance through Spiritual Warfare

The ministry opportunities, issues, and problems I have seen for over forty years in the church have been in the area of deliverance. I have watched where the area of deliverance is not being trained or addressed in the body of Christ. I have witnessed where people are searching to find who they can turn to in order to get help in all areas of deliverance.

Deliverance is Real

"Deliverance" is defined as the act of delivering or state of being delivered; as from bondage or danger. The act of releasing or rescuing someone in harm's way. The transfer of demonic spirits out of a person while liberating them from captivity. To serve a blow to an intended goal or target while providing freedom. To serve something promised or desired while obtaining freedom." (*Webster II New Riverside University Dictionary*, 359) "The act of setting a person free from oppression or depression while surrendering." (*Ministry Team Training Manual*, Randy Clark M-1)

God's desire is to remove us from the hand of the enemy (Isaiah 61:1). When we find ourselves in direct contact with the enemy, He enables us to defeat the enemy (Luke 10:19). God's total desire is that we would draw closer to Him (James 4:7.8).

In visiting several churches over the years, I have not seen the church face issues in the area of deliverance, and therefore they're not really meeting the needs of the body of Christ. Deliverance ministry seems almost nonexistent in churches today. I have personally witnessed many people suffering in bondage for years, not knowing that they could be liberated. It has been my privilege to train ministry teams around the world in aspects of deliverance ministry, yet I find that many people are still in captivity.

This has forged in me a burning desire to address the issue of deliverance, and that is what I intend to do in this book. The body of Christ needs to be educated on how to minister in the area of deliverance in the twenty-first century. In this book I will identify the ways in which deliverance ministry will assist believers in using what God has provided—for them to be set free in all areas of life, including land, property, and people.

When we study the subject of deliverance, it is helpful to look at the historical perspective: "Luther's and Calvin's interpretations of Christianity and their consequences during the middle decades of the 16th century, constitute the most radical new departures in history of old European Christianity. It was a matter of new thinking in Luther's case indeed, so new that it opened perspectives far beyond his own old European context of thought and life. That is something that will become clear when we consider modern European Christianity later in this book. In other words, it will become clear when we look at a manner of thinking among whose premises we shall not find such assertions as that the Bible delivers a full and correct description and explanation of history, geology, and astronomy; that Moses wrote the Pentateuch; that Israel's prophets predicted future things correctly; that the workings of the devil in human affairs can be clearly pointed out and that witches enter into covenants with him; That civil rights are Christian confessions that presuppose and condition each other; that heresy is something for the police to investigate; that the end of the world, with judgment, heaven and hell, is close at hand because such-and-such signs and portents appear. And above all, it will become clear when we consider the difference between whether the central religious problem is the existence of God or whether it is his state of mind toward—in Luther's words, 'me, lost and doomed creature that I am.'" (*The Story of Christianity,* Balling, Jacob, 197)

Luther's and Calvin's agreement during the sixteenth century identified that the devil had a hand in the affairs of mankind. They also agreed that human entities known as witches are used when they come into agreement with the devil through covenants. Through the formation of covenants that are established on earth and that have not been ordained by God, it brings curses upon the earth. Curses come when we come into agreement with the kingdom of darkness. When the curses are released, we find that we have to repent and reclaim the territory and land back for the glory of the Kingdom of God. The devil is not going to simply give back territory without a fight in the Spirit realm. This is accomplished via deliverance through spiritual warfare.

"By that we have touched on one of many aspects of the problems that occurred when European Christianity met non-European peoples. In the missionary movements of the nineteenth centuries, a message about God, the world, history, and conduct is brought to people with entirely different ideas and lifestyles. And it happens in close connection with an economic, political, and military expansion. How does that encounter turn out? In what manner is it expressed? One answer must be that liberation takes place, just as it always has at a transition to faith in Christ.

In the modern mission fields, as elsewhere, the central theme of Christianity, Christ's conquest of 'the powers' (death, demons, and despair) has been experienced as a living reality, even though there is no way of knowing which particular powers have plaqued the individual and how he or she has experienced the liberation." (*The Story of Christianity,* Balling, Jacob, 276)

Missionaries in the nineteenth century have also determined that people are under the influence of powers that are represented by demons, death, and despair. Missionaries also believe that people are to be liberated from their captivity. We see that the missionaries look at setting individuals free from the power of darkness. We see a picture of setting liberty to people who are in captivity. In the Global Mission Video "EE-TAW 1, Missionary Mark Zook faced what to do when he reached the Mouk Tribe that had never received the gospel. Zook looked at how the tribe viewed life; he studied their way of life to gain facts on the Mouk Tribe; how they lived with the constant fear of their ancestors. The missionary movement learned how their belief in the mask and dance was the spirit of their dead ancestors returning; how, if the Mouk women saw the mask, they were put to death. In the video, they showed the tradition of death in the Mouk Tribe portraying a man who died and when his wife saw the mask they carried her out to a far place, tied a rope around her neck and her body, and then they killed her. The Mouk woman had children who she left behind because of a belief. The Mouk woman was killed by her two brothers. What you truly believe affects what you do, and an action/belief can result in tragic consequences. Mark Zook started with a map to show the Mouk Tribe their geographical location, where they were and how Jesus traveled until he reached them in New Guinea.

"An example of a collective approach can be found in a report of how some Papua tribes in the interior of New Guinea decided on their conversion. According to the report, which is apt to remind us of what had happened in northern European mission fields 900 years earlier—the process began by the chiefs making known to their people with symbolic gestures, the choice they had to make between the evils that plagued them before they "Knew God"—tribal wars, sorcery, infanticide, and a life of freedom from such evils. Liberation was a wide concept often leading into new servitude under 'powers'—compulsory European dress and sexual practice, loss of old customs, and festivals that had secured daily life; surly moral supervision by missionaries." (*The Story of Christianity*, Jacob Balling, 276-277)

Nine hundred years ago, the Papua New Guinea tribes, through wars within the tribes prior to conversion, put them in bondage through land, property, and people under the influences of sorcery and the spirit of Molech where children were killed. When people and nations are in bondage, there is an oppressed society seeking to be free and liberated from the powers that hold them back from being who God designated them to be.

How to Deliver the Land That Was Taken Into Captivity through Spiritual Warfare

In the twentieth century, we looked at spiritual warfare through the eyes of an author named Dean Sherman, who wrote a book entitled *Spiritual Warfare for Every Christian*, describing how he was in Port Moresby, Papua New Guinea, and even though the people were being converted and coming to Christ, they were still bound by sin. Sherman describes how the Christians continued to practice witchcraft. When he preached against the practice of witchcraft and what they were doing, they became hardened.

God spoke to him. "One day as I lay praying on that rough floor, God's voice spoke into my mind. His answer was unexpected—something entirely new to my thinking. Yet it was as clear as I have ever heard Him speak: 'Praise is the key to breaking down the forces of darkness, which have held this city since the beginning of time. These forces have never been challenged.' I lay there stunned. I had never thought about spiritual forces controlling a place. No one I knew in 1970 was speaking about the powers of darkness over cities. I had never heard teaching on spiritual warfare, and was only aware of a few people who 'specialized' in ministries of delivering people from demons." (*Spiritual Warfare for Every Christian*, Dean Sherman, 11).

In the book of Isaiah 14:12-15, it says, "How art thou fallen from heaven, O Lucifer, Son of the morning! How art thou cut down to the ground, which didst weaken the nations! For thou hast said in thine heart, I will ascend into heaven, I will exalt my throne above the stars of God. I will sit also upon the mount of the congregation in the sides of the north! I will ascend above the heights of the clouds! I will be like the most high. Yet thou shalt be brought down to hell, to the sides of the pit." Lucifer was a Cherubim, who was close to God and served as a worshipping throne for God. Lucifer had reigned over the earth and the land of Eden. Lucifer's place of worship was located on the mountain of God, in the place called Salem, which is called Jerusalem today (Genesis 14). Abraham returned to Jerusalem, also called Salem where he paid tithes after the battle to Melchizedek.

Ezekiel 28:13-14, "Thou hast been in Eden the garden of God; every precious stone was thy covering, the sardius, topaz, and the diamond, the beryl, the onyx, and the jasper, the sapphire, the emerald, and the carbuncle, and gold; the workmanship of thy tabrets and of thy pipes was prepared in thee in the day that thou wast created. Thou art the anointed cherub that covereth; and I have set thee so, thou wast upon the holy mountain of God, thou hast walked up and down in the midst of the stones of fire." In the book of Ezekiel, we see a picture of God creating cherubim for his glory. When Lucifer was created, God also provided him with instruments of worship and sounds of heaven that came out of him. In the twenty-first century, we call these weapons of "Spiritual Warfare." The instruments, tabrets, and pipes are also used to conduct spiritual warfare (Psalm 150:3-5). "Praise him with the sound of the trumpet; praise him with the psaltery and harp, praise him with the timbrel (tambourine) and dance, praise him with stringed instruments and organs. Praise him upon the loud cymbals; praise him upon the high sounding cymbals." In the book of Joshua, God instructed Joshua to take the city of Jericho.

Joshua and his men of war march around the city of Jericho one time for six days. On the seventh day, God instructed Joshua and his men of war to take along with seven priests seven trumpets to go before the ark. The seven priests were to take seven trumpets of rams' horns and march seven times around Jericho. The people shouted and one long blast of the ram's horn brought the walls of the city of Jericho down. Lucifer lost his status as the worship leader in heaven when he fell and was cast into outer darkness from heaven. The war in heaven caused one third of the angels and Satan to fall. We now call these former angels demons and evil spirits.

The author Ron Phillips states, "What scientists call the Cambrian age was caused by the impact of God's judgment on Satan. Here we find the fossils of multitudes of ancient life forms. Though scientists call this time 'an explosion of life,' it was really 'an explosion of death.' The aftermath of the death of all those living creatures is the vast deposit of oil and gas that drives the world system and economy even now." (*Everyone's Guide to Demons and Spiritual Warfare*, Ron Phillips, 45).

We must begin with the fall of Adam and Eve in the Garden of Eden through which sin entered the world and mankind became separated from God. God had to have a plan first to create everything due to the fall of Satan. When God created everything with his son Jesus, due to the jealousy of Satan, he had another plan to redeem mankind back to him. God already knew that Satan would tempt Adam and Eve and they would fail. Meanwhile, while they were evicted from the Garden of Eden, God had to slay the first animal to provide clothing. He knew a lamb would have to be slain to redeem humanity back to God. When Adam and Eve ate of the tree of Knowledge of Good and Evil, they lost dominion and the land was cursed.

We see that sin continued throughout the Bible. When Cain and Abel grew up, God asked them to provide worship to Him. Only Abel's worship was accepted because he brought the first fruits to God. Cain was rejected because he brought leftovers for worship and not his first fruits. Cain eventually killed Abel and denied it, but the blood of Abel cried out to God. We see the sin of Cain, killing his brother Abel and burying him on the land, bringing forth the death spirit of the blood of Abel as it cried out to God. We can see why the death of 5 billion aborted babies around the world cry out daily to God. We now see a picture of so much sin on the earth that as we get to the book of Genesis, we see that God found only eight righteous people. God has to now build an Ark through Noah and kill all the people in the world except for two of each animal and Noah and his family. We see a picture of how each time sin has entered in that it destroys. God has had to step in with a plan of spiritual warfare to restore and create all things new.

Even with things created new through Noah and his family, sin still abounded and man was cursed through his nakedness and drunkenness until true worship was restored through Seth. Joseph saved a nation called Israel today from famine by becoming second in command to Pharaoh and moving them into Goshen. Moses was born after the Pharaoh, who knew Joseph, died. Moses survived Pharaoh killing male newborns and became the deliverer that led the nation of Israel out of 400 years of bondage from Egypt into the wilderness. God used ten plagues against Pharaoh as spiritual warfare to deliver the nation of Israel out of the hands of the Egyptians. God fought the army of Egypt through spiritual warfare. God created a pillar of fire to hold them back, which gave Israel a head start to cross the Red Sea. God defeated the army of Egypt by closing the Red Sea on them.

A True Life Scenario

During a scheduled assistance visit to a cell group church located in Kentucky, a lawyer named John asked if when we came to visit if we could help them reclaim the territory and some property that was defiled by the enemy. John was given a building by God and was instructed by God to keep the building because eventually it would become a Healing Center for all nations to come through.

God hid us from the enemy so that we could scope out the area to see what was going on, before the enemy knew we were upon the territory of the kingdom of darkness. When we entered the meeting location, there was a very strong spirit of death in the place. I asked the owner of the property if there was a recent death. The owner of the property had lost her son to a motorcycle accident within the past two months. I followed the Holy Spirit and, with the permission of the owner, went straight to the place in the closet where the spirit of death was hiding. The motorcycle helmet of the son, which carried the spirit of death, was sitting on the shelf. The helmet carried the spirit of death. I took the time to break the spirit of death off of the object. Then it was safe for the family to keep as a remembrance without spirits attached.

The assistance team consisted of four members providing service to the cell group church. We provided assistance by first looking over the members to see how they were doing. What we found was that many of them had to be revived because they were exhausted and defeated through the spiritual warfare. Many of the cell group church members wanted to quit, so we had to minister to them and resurrect their spirits before we could use them in spiritual warfare. I began to use the spiritual warfare weapon of worship to minster and have the cell group church army revived. I began to teach them how they must enter into praise because the battle belonged to the Lord. Additionally, through worship, they would renew their strength while waiting on the strategies from heaven on how to take the territory back.

I proceeded to bang a tambourine and shook it to break off all the witchcraft that had overcome the cell group church members. Once I began to bang the tambourine, the enemy knew we were in the area. The meeting place was visited by a witch assigned by the warlocks who came to the meeting place. As long as the worship music played, the witch could not stay inside the house. The witch kept running outside because of the presence of the Holy Spirit. The Holy Spirit was so strong through the worship and tambourine patterns that she stayed away. The enemy sent her there to eavesdrop and carry information back to their headquarters as to why we were there.

The next day we were up at the crack of dawn. We went down to the facilities that had been defiled by the enemy. Across the street was a government building, and on the right side of the building was a cemetery. Behind the building was the area where the witches' and warlocks' coven faced. God had shown us all these things in the spirit the night before, so we knew what we had to do to clean up the building. I brought twelve large bottles of extra virgin olive oil, grape juice, and communion to take back the land. I had new flags made that had never been used. We took praise and worship music into the building that was defiled. We began the spiritual warfare of cleansing the land by pouring oil on the land where the Healing Center was located and reclaimed that territory. We went to the cemetery and reclaimed that area by blessing the land with oil and prayer. God led us to pray over the government building for all the corruption that was going on so as to seal what we would accomplish that day in taking the entire territory for God.

Once the land was recovered, we went into the building and found demonic pentagrams painted on the floor. We went from area to area and God revealed where incest to little girls had occurred in the building. As we went further into the building, we found graffiti where demonic threats from the witches' and warlocks' covens had covered the walls. We started from the back of the building cleansing and praying with oil throughout the entire building. We repented and renounced the defilement in every category; such as molestation, rape, incest, blood sacrifices, and animalism that was done in each room of the building that was shown to us by God.

Once the building was completely cleansed and repentance was accomplished in each room, we washed over the entire building with oil including the water tunnel we found. We poured oil into the water tunnel when God revealed what had occurred for sacrifices in there. When we arrived at the front door's walk-in entrance where the pentagram was drawn on the floor, we poured oil and walked around it, we repented, and after the eighth walk around, God said to open the door. When we did, there was a mass exodus of screaming demons. Next, angels from heaven came streaming in by the thousands to secure the facilities. I had to duck as the demons were leaving and the angels of the Lord Jesus Christ came in. We could barely stand, there were so many angels and the Presence was strong in the building. We proceeded to hand out flags with significant meaning— the blood of Jesus, the father's heart, purity, prosperity, royalty, gold, deity, and the peace of Jerusalem. We also proceeded to play praise and worship music and take communion to seal the presence and the spiritual defeat of the powers of darkness over the territory with God.

How to Deliver Personal Property That Has Fallen Under a Curse

The problem with objects: "Once we become aware of spiritual darkness, we can begin looking around in our homes and see what we own that does not bring glory to God. What we mean by this phrase is something that, by its very nature, can attract or be inhabited by darkness."

Foreign gods: "You shall not make for yourself any carved image or any likeness of anything that is in heaven above, or that is in the earth beneath, or that is in the water under the earth" (Deuteronomy 5:8). In this passage, the second of the Ten Commandments, "a carved image" refers to any tangible object that represents an idol, god, or demonic figure. Not only is this a welcome mat for demonic activity, but also God hates it. Though it may be out of ignorance, it is surprising to realize how many Christians have such items in their homes.

"These objects include Buddhas (as was on Pam's jewelry box; Pam is Chuck Pierce's wife whose jewelry box was purchased in Thailand), Hindu images, fertility gods or goddesses (or any type of gods or goddess); Egyptian images; Greek gods; gargoyles; Kachina dolls, totem poles, or any other Native American figures that depict or glorify a spirit or demonic being; evil depictions of creatures such as lions, dogs, dragons, or cats (or any other creature made with demonic distortions); or any other image of a person, idol, god, or demonic figure that is considered an object of worship or spiritual power in any culture in the world.

On trips, many people collect these types of artifacts as souvenirs without understanding their significance—much like the jewelry box that came from Thailand." (*Protecting Your Home from Spiritual Darkness,* Chuck D. Pierce and Rebecca Wagner Systema, 32-33).

How Deliverance Works

It is recommended that we look around and do some spiritual cleansing when we think that there are constant battles going on in our homes and/or on our personal property. Begin by asking God what is the cause of all the spiritual warfare that you are encountering. God will begin to reveal to you what cursed object came into your home or personal property. Many people are unaware of the battles they are faced with and having to fight because they don't take time to do some spiritual house cleaning.

Take your car for a check-up to ensure that it continues to run smoothly on a quarterly or six-month basis. Take time to look at the items in your home and your personal property to ensure no intrusion has occurred, so that you can live in peace with the presence of God in your life and home.

False Religions: "Objects or materials related to false religions, such as Mormonism, Islam, Jehovah's Witness, Hinduism, Eastern Religions, Christian Science, Native religions, Baha's and so forth, need to be carefully evaluated. This includes instruction books on Yoga, transcendental meditation, mantras, and so on.

Occult Objects: "Anything related to the occult must be destroyed completely. These objects include Ouija boards, good luck charms, amulets, astrology items (including horoscopes); tarot cards, crystals; fetishes; water witching sticks; Voodoo dolls; pagan symbols; crystal balls; any ritual item, such as a mask, a pyramid, or an obelisk; any item obtained from occult or Voodoo shops; any item related to black magic, fortune telling, palmistry; demon worship; spirit guides; witchcraft; Satanism, or New Age. None of these items or any other such item should have any place in the Christian home." (*Protecting Your Home from Spiritual Darkness,* Pierce and Systema, 33-34).

People who were once serving in the occult and have been taken out of these practices need to look around their home and personal property to see if there are still some of these religious objects lying around in garages, basements, attics, or storage sheds. Whether we are aware or unaware of these objects lying around, we are still giving access to demonic presence over these objects and to our family members.

We need to look and see if we have things packed away in the closets of our homes. We must also look in the most obvious places. If you have a rebellious youth living at home, check out their rooms to see if they have brought some of the occult objects into your home.

Secret-Society Objects: "Secret societies, such as Freemasonry, Shriners, Eastern Star, Job's Daughters, Odd Fellows, Elks, Amaranth, DeMolay, Rainbow for Girls or Daughters of the Nile, often require their members to take oaths and go through initiation rituals, including pledging allegiance to various deities, which are completely contrary to God's Word. Because that is the case, demons can easily attach themselves to items, such as books, rings, aprons, regalia, and memorabilia that represent these societies. Additionally, because such items are often passed down through family lines, there is a generational issue that must be dealt with." (*Protecting Your Home from Spiritual Darkness,* Pierce and Systema, 34).

We have spent a lot of time educating families on the dangers of keeping some of these objects in their home because it has caused a host of problems. Many objects have been handed down within a family's ancestry that they are unaware of. There are dangers in their homes that they have opened their families to, but once these objects are removed and burned, it will liberate the home, personal property, and the family.

I mentioned that these objects must be burned because of the demonic powers of the oaths taken and the demon's presence in the objects. When we destroy it by fire, it will prevent the transferring of the demonic powers to others.

I was asked by a friend named Donna to come and look at some personal property that they were going to rent. They had not yet moved all of their personal items into the house. I took a team of five people with me on a Sunday to look at the property. I went into the house and found all kinds of spirits from the previous tenants. With permission, I looked at the property outside. In the back yard, I saw two choke points on the land. The Holy Spirit took me to the two places that were cursed and had high points on the land. Immediately, I took Donna outside to the locations and showed her where there were curses placed and laid on the land (Genesis 3:17 and Deuteronomy. 28:18). I had not realized that all the people I took with me had never worked on taking back personal property before. On the spot, I provided a crash course to the team of how to take back personal property. I proceeded to take the team to the two areas outside that were cursed and began to repent (Matthew 3:2, and Acts 2:38) for the curses that were placed on the land. We asked God to cleanse the land and we blessed the areas.

We poured oil (Exodus 29:21) into the two areas that were cleansed. Donna prayed over the area, because she needed to know how to take back the land where she was dwelling. We took the team and proceeded to cleanse every room in the home. When we arrived in our first room, there was a molestation spirit in that room, and we repented for what was done to the child on the property; we asked God to forgive it. We opened the window, and the spirit fled the room. Then we were free to play praise and worship music; we proceeded to anoint the windows and the furniture in the room, and we blessed the room. We prophesied what God instructed us in each room as we walked through and cleansed the home.

When we arrived in the living room, there were heavy spirits of pornography and perversion. We proceeded to repent for the sinful things that entered into that home. God said to open the front door, and the spirits of pornography and perversion left. I followed those spirits out to ensure that they did not linger in the yard or at the door. God said to anoint the door outside and inside. When our team repented, renounced, anointed, and prophesied in each room, we took communion to seal the work that was completed.

Before we began the process, we had discussed that we would pray and fast during this entire process until the job was done. We did this so that if we encountered any principalities that we could defeat them, because our flesh was down and we had spiritual ears to clearly hear what God wanted done in each room.

When renting or purchasing property, ask God before moving in if it is the right place. I have seen people move into places that have had all kinds of principalities and powers of darkness on their personal property as well as the territory. I knew when I arrived that they did not pray or ask God if they should move there.

In another case, property which was purchased had had a history of rape and incest involving a woman and children. The property is a church building in the state of Illinois that was abandoned and foreclosed. I was asked by the church leader who purchased the property if I would assist in taking back the territory, which included taking back the personal property for the church.

We had a group of five people for the job, and one person on the team raised doubts in my spirit. During the entire process, I had a check in my spirit that this person was still under the influence of demonic powers. I asked the owner if she would ask her to leave in order for this mission to be a success. As a rule of thumb, when selecting people to do deliverance through spiritual warfare, especially on personal property, I must ensure that they are not possessed by any demons. When you take people who are possessed, you're setting yourself up for mission failure. The team should be made up of successful, stable people who are free and walking in the authority delegated to them by Jesus Christ.

We proceeded to cleanse the building using praise and worship music so as to drive out the principalities that had settled in the territory and the property. We asked God for strategic plans on how to take this place back. God's instruction was to begin with repentance and forgiveness for what had transpired against the women and children in this place (Matthew 3:2, Acts 2:38). When we finished repenting for the women and children, God said to sweep through the building with flags (Psalm 20:5, Psalm 60:4, Song of Solomon 2:4). We used several flags whose names signify what was being restored to the region and the church—the Army of God flags, Freedom flags, Father Heart of God flag, Purity flag, red flag representing the Blood of Jesus and the Alpha and Omega flags (Song of Solomon 6:10, Song of Solomon 6:4, Isaiah 13:2).

By holding something in your hand, lifted up in praise, you will establish the name of the Lord on high. When lifted up, it establishes a landmark so the world may know that Christ is King. It enforces the standard against the enemy as warfare takes place in the heavenlies. Isaiah 59:19 says, "So shall they fear the name of the Lord from the west, and His glory from the rising of the sun, when the enemy comes in like a flood, the Spirit of the Lord will lift up a standard against him." (*Praise Him with the Tambourine and Dance Yap*, Magrate, 27)

In Exodus 17:15, we read, "And Moses built an altar and called its name, The Lord is my Banner (Jehovah Nissi)." John 12:32 says, "And I, if I am lifted up from the earth, will draw all peoples to myself."

One should not do this unless instructed by God and called to this level of spiritual warfare. I was asked by God to climb up on the roof of the building, and I was to wave the Blood of Jesus and the Purity flags on the roof of the building. I had to climb up a ladder that got me up on the roof. I walked the entire roof of the building while waving the flags violently. I saw the principalities leaving the building screaming and the demons leaving the territory.

"Raise a banner! When we are in the army, our troops will have a flag or a banner to show its allegiance to a kingdom and to proclaim its advance. We are in a kingdom; we are in an army, and we are advancing." (*The Sword and the Tambourine Farwell*, Hanna E. 177-178)

I waved the flags on the roof for approximately thirty minutes with the help of the Holy Spirit, and I watched the angels coming on the roof and into the territory in record numbers. We finished taking back the territory from the kingdom of darkness, and we anointed the facilities with oil; we prayed the presence of God and his Kingdom back into the church. We finished sealing the work that was done by breaking bread and sharing communion.

David's return to Ziklag revealed that the Amalekites had burned it with fire and carried away their wives, sons, and daughters into captivity. David inquired of God whether he should pursue the Amalekites. God granted David permission to pursue and take the Amalekites and recover all that was stolen (1 Samuel 30).

How to Deliver People Who Are Under Attack and Tormented By the Enemy

"For the weapons of our warfare are not carnal but mighty through God to the pulling down of strongholds; Casting down imaginations, and every high thing that exalted itself against the knowledge of God, and bringing into captivity every thought to the obedience of Christ" (2 Corinthians 10: 4-5).

Why We Need To Know What to Do in Deliverance

Emotional problems: "In my experience one type of spiritual stronghold is manifested through severe emotional problems. Not all emotional problems are strongholds, but they may be when emotional disturbances recur repeatedly. During those times, there seems to be no permanent cure or relief from them; in other words, they persist in the life and personality of an individual.

Some of the most common symptoms of this stronghold are anger, depression, fear, feelings of inferiority, feelings of insecurity, feelings of rejection (feeling unwanted and unloved, hatred, jealousy, resentment, self-pity, and worry." (*A Divine Revelation of Spiritual Warfare,* Mary K. Baxter and Dr. T.L. Lowery, 59-60).

Emotional problems play a large role when people are under attack and are being tormented by the enemy. If one is not stable during the attack, the enemy will try to wipe you out depending on how deep he can take you in any category of emotions that you displayed while being tormented.

Mental problems: "Another spiritual stronghold is the stifling grip of mental problems. These problems occur through disturbances in the mind or in the thought life. Caused by distorted thinking, this stronghold of evil brings about mental torment. It manifests itself in unrealistic and unexplained procrastination, incomprehensible indecision, wavering, compromise, confusion, delusions, doubt, rationalization, and even the loss of memory."

Disruptive speech: "Satan also builds spiritual strongholds in the lives of individuals through disruptive speech. This stronghold may be revealed in uncontrolled outbursts that occur suddenly and without warning. Yet it often manifests itself through lying, profanity, blasphemy, criticism, mockery, railing, and gossip." (*A Divine Revelation of Spiritual Warfare*, Baxter and Dr. Lowery, 60)

The symptoms of mental problems and disruptive speech are provided so you can see what the warning signs look like and how to begin to combat what the enemy is trying to do to your family members or loved ones through spiritual warfare. Many people go through life under constant attack and torment not knowing what they can do to defeat the enemy in the fight for their lives. If you are unaware of what to look for, then you must learn to recognize the symptoms so you are armed. The enemy is dangerous and for you to take on the enemy and fight for your loved ones, you must know what to do when they're attacked and tormented.

The last three categories I want to identify are sexual problems, addictions, and physical infirmities.

Sexual problems: "Another form of spiritual oppression is often seen today in the stronghold of sexual problems. This includes, but is not limited to, recurring unclean thoughts and impure sexual acts. It may include fantasy sexual experiences, masturbation, lust, provocative and lewd behavior, homosexuality, fornication, adultery, incest, and other perversions."

Addictions: "The enemy wants to destroy as many souls as he can, and he has found that addictions are an effective weapon to use. Satan loves to oppress people through dependence on such things as nicotine, alcohol, illegal drugs, prescription and over-the-counter medications, gambling, television, the Internet, caffeine, and even food, including salt and sugar. Therefore, what some psychologists and psychiatrists call an 'addictive personality' may actually be the result of a spiritual stronghold."

Physical infirmities: "While not all physical infirmities are strongholds, God revealed to me that a number of diseases and physical afflictions are due to spirits of infirmity. When a demon of infirmity is cast out, there is often the need to pray for healing of whatever damage has resulted. A close and necessary relationship exists between deliverance and healing." (*A Divine Revelation of Spiritual Warfare*, Baxter and Dr. Lowery, 60-61)

In the twenty-first century, not only is the world having problems in these areas, but leaders who are representing our nations, as well as in the churches, are being reported on the news of the hidden areas that are being revealed as problems in their lives. If we don't take time to deal with the sexual problems, addictions, and physical infirmities, we could lose many of our leaders to the hand of the enemy. The most important thing to prevent sexual problems and addictions is that we must become aware and look at the symptoms early on before the fall. John 10:10, says, "The thief cometh not, but for to steal, and to kill, and to destroy: I am come that they might have life, and that they might have it more abundantly."

I have had many people ask me how they can stop the attack on their children when they are sleeping at night and are being tormented by the enemy. I ask the parents what the children are seeing at night that frightens them. I ask the parents when the children's sleeping patterns began to change. Was there any foreign object that was brought into the house, or did the child see something on television or in the movies that brought on the nightmares? When I pray for delivery over children, it is usually revealed to me that the children are seeing demons in their rooms and are unable to sleep. With the parents present, I begin to speak to the tormenting demon to leave the child, and then I break off the demons that were assigned to harass the child.

I also ask that when the parents go home, that they open the window and command the demons to leave the room. Then I instruct the parents to anoint the windows and the doors to the room and the bed that the child sleeps in so they can continue to rest peacefully.

I have had times when I delivered children through prayers with the parents where I sent angelic angels to sweep the place of any demon's stronghold in the place, and I have sent the blood of Jesus to their homes. I have had reports from the parents that the demon left and their child or children are resting peacefully. When we wait on the Holy Spirit to guide us on what to do for each situation that occurs, we will see victory and breakthroughs for everyone seeking deliverance.

People have asked me to go to their homes because there is constant attack and torment on their families. I always initially look at when things changed from the normal pattern of their living on a daily basis. I have found that when they are constantly battling in their minds, and when there is continual confusion and they don't know what's going on, that these are warning signs. It's the beginning of the attacks that usually escalates to tormenting by the enemy. It will depend on how long they allowed the attacks to occur in their home and over their family. I find that early detection is crucial to an early defeat before the battle escalates over a family. If the family has any doors open among themselves or others, they have to close the doors first. Only then can we go after the enemy once the doors are shut.

How Spiritual Weapons are Used by Deliverance through Spiritual Warfare

"Finally, my brethren be strong in the lord, and in the power of his might. Put on the whole armour of God that ye may be able to stand against the wiles of the devil. For we wrestle not against flesh and blood, but against principalities, against powers, against the rulers of the darkness of the world, against spiritual wickedness in high places. Wherefore take unto you the whole armour of God that ye may be able to withstand in the evil day and having done all, to stand. Stand therefore, having your loins girt about with truth, and having on the breastplate of righteousness: And your feet shod with the preparation of the gospel of peace. Above all, taking the shield of faith, wherewith ye shall be able to quench all the fiery darts of the wicked. And take the helmet of salvation, and the sword of the Spirit, which is the word of God" (Ephesians 6: 10 -17).

As soldiers in the army of God, when we look at the armor of God, we must understand that we are at war. We are not fighting in the natural like we do when we go to war against another nation; we are fighting a spiritual battle. God has given us all the tools we need to win the war. In order to maintain victory as the army of God, we must put on the armor of God. How do we put on the armor of God? We need to understand the spiritual battle we are fighting. When we exercise the armor, we do it by praying (Philippians 4:6) and studying the Word of God, (2 Timothy

2:15) fasting, (Luke 2:37) fellowship, (Acts 2:42), and through praise and worship. The way we exercise the spiritual weapons is through using the Name of Jesus (Matthew 18:20) and then we exercise the delegated authority given to us by Jesus. We stand in the battle by knowing the enemy's limitations, method of attack, and his schemes. When we put on the breastplate of righteousness, we must ensure that we are not striving for the approval of God. We must confirm that we are doing the will of God and not our will. We must protect our heart from the attack of the enemy when we are hurt or offended. The enemy stands daily accusing us, but we must remember that our righteousness was purchased through Jesus Christ's death on the cross.

When we study the feet being shod with the preparation of the gospel of peace, we must put on peace. We do this by going forth and preaching the good news so that others have an opportunity to receive Jesus Christ as Lord and Savior in their lives. We must be willing to preach the Word of God even if the Word is not accepted when we go. We are the only ones to carry the peace of God to nations around the world. We also take the peace when we travel to our places of employment and our neighborhoods. We walk in the shoes of peace with God. We carry and take territory for the Kingdom of God. So if we are not doing our part by going and taking the peace of God, we are not exercising our feet shod with the preparation of the gospel of peace. (John 14:27, Romans 16:20, Psalm 18:33) When we put on our belt of truth, we can wield the sword of the Spirit by using the Word of God (Hebrews 4:12) against the enemy. The sword of the Spirit only works when we open up the Word of God and spend time finding out what is available to us through the Word of God. We need to know the truth of the Word of God from the lies of the enemy. When we take on the shield of faith, we must exercise our faith once we are filled with the Word of God.

If our faith is not tested, it cannot be trusted. God said in this life we will have tests, trials, and persecutions, but we are to be of good cheer because Jesus has overcome. Our promotion comes through being tested in life. We cannot handle the things of the kingdom if we do not know how to defeat the enemy at each new level, and God will not promote (Psalm 75:6-7). The helmet of salvation is where we have to learn how to transform our mind and the way we think about fighting in spiritual warfare (Romans 1:28, Romans 8:6, Ephesians 4:17). We must not allow our mind to be confused or careless of hearing the false words of the kingdom of darkness. We must protect our minds to be stayed on Christ Jesus, the author and finisher and developer of our faith. We must renew our minds daily through prayer and the Word of God. We need to not conform our thinking and doing to the things the world is doing that do not line up with the Kingdom of God. We cannot fight in the natural, but we must fight as we are led by God through the Holy Spirit. The devil has had thousands of years in fighting, but we must depend totally on God.

"Spiritual Warfare: Yesterday and Today—Spiritual warfare did not begin with the human race; it began with the rebellion of the angels. These powerful and magnificent created beings possess an intellect and will similar to human beings but different from them in one vital respect—man is uniquely made in the image and likeness of God. Angels are special creatures, since they dwell in heaven and were created as ministering spirits, but human beings are exclusively God's children, since we bear His image (Hebrews 1:7). People are important to God, or He would have abandoned us to the destruction we so richly deserved as a punishment for our rebellion. But instead of destroying man, God provided a way of escape." (*The Kingdom of the Occult,* Martin Walter, Rische Martin, Jill, and Gorden Van Kurt, 589)

The first step you must take before you go into any battle is to ensure that you have no sin in your life, and if you do, you must close the door to that sin. You must also make sure that you have a relationship with Father God, the Son and the Holy Spirit. If these first two steps are not in place in your life, then you will be defeated by the enemy. The third area is that you must have the Word of God planted in you. When you go to face your opponent in a spiritual battle, the enemy knows if you have the Word, which is your sword of the spirit or not. Many Christians want to fight in a spiritual battle with no Word inside their inner man. An empty vessel has nothing to throw at the enemy during the battle. A full vessel has so much that it pours it out and it defeats the enemy instantly in a spiritual battle. You must pray and fast before you enter the spiritual battle so you can get the strategies from heaven for each assignment you take on for the Kingdom of God. Remember, you are not fighting the battle, but the Holy Spirit of God is fighting through you.

You must be submitted to authority in order to have authority in the battle. If you are a Lone Ranger out there with no spiritual covering fighting battles, the enemy knows that you have no covering, and you will end up like the seven sons of Sceva. Acts 19: 14, "And there were seven sons of one Sceva, a Jew, and chief of the priests, which did so..." Acts 19:15, "And the evil spirit answered and said, Jesus I know, and Paul I know; but who are ye?" Acts 19:16, "And the man in whom the evil spirit was leaped on them, and overcame them, and prevailed against them, so that they fled out of that house naked and wounded."

The weapons that you must carry for the attack: Rule number one is that you are on the offense taking back what was stolen. Do not fight the spiritual battle on the defensive; you are not defending; you are running the enemy out of the territory. Remember, he is the trespasser not you. Therefore, your job is to kick him out through spiritual warfare. You must pray before you go into spiritual warfare. You must praise. Therefore, take music and a device that can play the music, so that praise and worship music is flowing while you are fighting a spiritual battle. The enemy hates worship, and he flees where there is praise and worship.

When we spend time praying and singing praises of worship to our God, we give glory to Him. God loves it when we pray and praise him. Psalm 100:1-2 says we are to make a joyful noise unto the lord. When we spend time praying and praising, we show that we trust God for the outcome of victory even before we see the end results. When we pray and praise, we are developing an intimate relationship with the father. We are to draw nigh to God and he will draw nigh to us as we pray and praise him. God wants us to resist the enemy and we do it when we spend time coming into prayer and praise. Prayer and praise changes things. When we don't pray and praise God, we don't get the results we are looking for to change situations that are not in agreement with the Kingdom of God. God is always looking to see who will stand in the gap, and when we pray and praise, we are standing in the gap so that we can be used by God. God is looking for vessels unto honor that are willing to serve. When we enter into prayer and praise, we are saying, "Here I am, Lord; I am willing to sacrifice my flesh to enter into a time of prayer and praise with You to see what is on the heart of the Father to share in the suffering of the Father for the injustices that are on the earth." When we pray and praise, we are being used by God to change the circumstances and situations in life that do not please God.

The worship also ushers the presence of the Lord into the area you are taking back in the spiritual battle. When we look at the presence of

God in worship, we have to go back to the tabernacle. God used Moses to design the tabernacle according to the pattern in heaven so that the Israelites would be able to have a place where God could come and inhabit and live among his people (Exodus 25:8). The tabernacle was a picture of the people coming to worship and ushering in the presence of God (Exodus 25-40). The Levitical priesthood that was newly assigned was responsible to see the worship incorporated to God. God brought the Israelites out of Egypt so that they could worship him in Mount Sinai. God created us for worship and to bring glory to God. We worship and bring in the presence through silence, (Ecclesiastes 3:7) and gazing, (Psalm 46:10).

The presence of the Lord is in each and every one of us. When we are born again, we receive the comforter and we become carriers of the presence of God. So we are created in the image and likeness of God (Genesis 1:26). We can see today how the tabernacle is now the Holy Spirit, and when we become saved we receive the baptism of the Holy Spirit. We are now full-time worshippers because we are carriers of the presence of God. Wherever we go, we take the presence of God with us. We no longer have to go out to the tent of meeting (Numbers 3-4), but we now have the presence of the Holy Spirit living in us. When we enter into worship, we are entering into the presence of the King Jesus.

We must take small or large flags, streamers, Shofar and tambourines into battle. If you have portable drums, bring those along as well. The Shofar and flags release the angels of God into a city, state, region, territory, or nation (Psalm 20:5, Psalm 60:4, Isaiah 13: 2-3, Daniel 10:11-13, Joshua 6: 3-5, 15, 20). The tambourine stops the enemy in his tracks, and based on the patterns used in spiritual warfare, there is restoration, full gospel, through Christ, combat, horse and rider, and many others. These are patterns that restore and release things into territories that were stolen by the enemy. If we are reclaiming territory, we want to wash it with anointing oil and finish with sharing communion.

Chapter Two
Two Kingdoms

"In whom the god of this world hath blinded the minds of them which believe not" (2 Corinthians 4:4).

How the Two Kingdoms Work

Satan is also called the god of this world. Satan has established a ruling hierarchy on earth, and he operates out of four kingdoms on the earth today. These kingdoms are in the spirit realm. The Western Kingdom of the spirit realm is headquartered in the city of Rome, Italy. The Eastern Kingdom is located in Saudi Arabia where they go to worship in the city of Mecca. The Southern Kingdom is located in Sydney, Australia, and the Northern Kingdom is found in Moscow, the Soviet Union headquarters. Satan also has both spirited beings and human beings working together. Satan promotes them so as to keep people satisfied in order to keep them working for him. Satan has field marshals and they possess extreme power. The four are called Apollyon, Greek (Revelation 9:11) Abaddon, Hebrew

(Revelation 9:11), Belial, and the Beast. (Revelation 13: 2-18). They are extremely wicked and powerful. Here is where he is a smart ruler; he has them equal so they don't overthrow him as he tries to overthrow God in the Kingdom of God. These four are called principalities in the kingdom of darkness. (*Mysterious Secrets of The Dark Kingdom*, J.P. Timmons, 97)

God's kingdom is made up of Cherubim, Seraphim, archangels (warring angels), and angels (ministering angels). When compared, the counterfeit effect of the kingdom of darkness to the Kingdom of God is obvious. The Cherubim were angels that protected the Ark of the Covenant. "The Cherubim are symbolic of guardianship as seen at the gate of Eden in Genesis 3:24. They were here seen to protect the untainted and absolute holiness of God, as He is seen in the mercy seat dwelling among His people." (*The Tabernacle,* H.B. McGowan, 130) "Cherubim heavenly beings, described as having multiple wings and both human and animal form. They are presented in Scripture as directly serving God. Carved representations of cherubim were placed on the Ark of the Covenant, and they were embroidered on the tabernacle's curtains. Solomon's Temple contained huge figures of cherubim. Seraphim heavenly beings, mentioned only in Isaiah's vision of God, Isaiah 6." Seraphim are evidently similar to, or possibly the same as the cherubim mentioned elsewhere in the Bible." (*What the Bible is all About Bible Handbook,* Dr. Henrietta C. Mears, 691,706) You find the Seraphim are protecting the throne of God, a job that Lucifer once had. The archangels protect nations like Israel, and Michael the Archangel is in the forefront of protecting Israel. "Angels heavenly beings created by God before He created Adam and Eve. Angels act as God's messengers to men and women. They also worship God." (*What the Bible is all About Bible Handbook;* Dr. Henrietta C. Mears, 687.) Angels were sent to minster as shown in the Bible (Luke 1:26-38) when the Angel Gabriel went to both Mary and then to Zechariah to tell him that his wife Elisabeth would have a son and he would be called John. After Jesus was led by the Spirit into the wilderness to be tempted by the devil (Matthew 4:1), and when the temptation was completed, angels came to minister to Jesus (Matthew 4:11).

How the Chain Of Command Works In Both Kingdoms

Apollyon's main function is to promote false religion. His primary goal in the kingdom of darkness is to turn people away from God into idolatry. Apollyon wants to keep us from thinking about God. Apollyon wants to keep us from reading the Bible and praying. Apollyon wants us to go to hell and keeps us from doing anything for God. Abaddon is a tall, black, and foul-smelling demon whose presence is found in homosexuals. Abaddon is called the polluting demon in Africa. Abaddon's goal is to pollute the human race. He is in charge of polluting and corrupting habits in smoking, cocaine, and other drugs, rock music, pornography, homosexuality, fornication, incest, bestiality, pedophilia, and alcohol. Abaddon is the demon that encourages sexual immorality. (*Mysterious Secrets of the Dark Kingdom,* J.P. Timmons, 101,103.)

In the book of Exodus, chapters 32 and 33, we see an example of the Israelites who were liberated out of bondage for 400 years. When the Israelites were left by Moses in the wilderness, they became restless (Exodus 32:1). God called Moses up to Mount Sinai to commune with Him. The Israelites asked Aaron to build them gods to worship. The price the Israelites paid was that 3,000 of them lost their lives for worshiping idols and many were plagued.

Growing up in an inner city (urban) environment, I witnessed many people in the early 1970s that were into the drugs, alcohol, violence, gangs, prostitution, and shooting scene. Many teens, young adults, and grownups had lost their way. With the loss of identification, many of the people chose to live in the harsh circumstances of their lifestyle. When I was growing up, I had an uncle who was into the lifestyle of drugs and alcohol. The Lord provided me an opportunity to see how the drugs were heated up in a little stove and then put into a needle where they took a rubber band and tied it to their arms to shoot the cocaine and other drugs into their arms. Although I didn't participate in any of these things, God provided me a chance to see what I was dealing with so I could liberate the teens and young adults involved in the Youth in Action program and help them get their life back on track.

Many of the teens and youth were involved in prostitution—selling their bodies so they could purchase the drugs they needed. God allowed me an opportunity to look at the kingdom of darkness through my uncle who happened to be at all these locations in the inner city. My uncle was not saved at the time. I saw how they rolled marijuana into white sheets of paper and make it so that it looked like cigarettes. Eventually my uncle contracted HIV through a dirty needle and accepted Jesus Christ before he died. God granted me a chance to save many lives out of this lifestyle and put them back on the road to recovery and success. Many teens and youth were taken out of detention facilities and placed back into schools. The young adults were able to be restored and successfully placed back in college and in the workforce.

Belial is often called the god of the planet. Belial's main job is to cause war and death. He likes to destroy people and see them die. Belial works with Magog, the god of war, who reports to Belial. The two work together in the kingdom of darkness to cause bloodshed and provide blood for the demon world. The Beast is Satan's end time weapon. He will be used on a massive scale to deceive mankind and cause bloodshed, false worship, and much destruction. The Beast will cause wide-scale destruction and desolation for the human race during the end times and his number is 666.

Under the four principalities are eight powers. They are called Ashtaroth; Baal, Magog, Beelzebub, Asmodee, Mammon, Paimon, and

Ariton. The powers and principalities meet with Satan once a month on the last Friday of each month. (*Mysterious Secrets of The Dark Kingdom,* J.P. Timmons, 115.)

In the Book of I Samuel 15:1-35, King Saul was given instruction by God to destroy the Amalekites, every man, woman, and child, all their sheep, cattle and donkeys and to keep certain things that were consecrated unto the Lord. King Saul was disobedient in this, and it caused Samuel to have to kill the Amalekite King to fulfill the request of the Lord. In the book of Joshua, God gives instruction to Israel to go in and take the city of Jericho, killing all except Rahab and her family. The city of Jericho was burnt to the ground. In the book of Genesis 14:12-16, Lot was taken into captivity and all his family to include the goods he owned. Abraham, armed with 318 servants, went into battle to defeat the four kings who took advantage of Lot and his family. Abraham restored all back to Lot by going to war against the four kings and defeating them. God will require his people to go to war when it is to defeat the wicked people in order to stop evil from prevailing. Blood that was shed in Biblical times were to root out wickedness in the land.

Ashtaroth is called the Queen of Heaven and is also known as the goddess of fertility (Jeremiah 7:18, 44; 17-19, 25.) The Queen of Heaven works with Baal; they work with the principalities. Apollyon works in the promotion of false religion. Ashtaroth is in charge of all the nature religions that we call paganism. "The ancient Moon Goddess (sometimes referred to in literature by the masculine 'Moon God') has exerted a good bit of influence over peoples of the Middle East for millennia. The spiritual powers behind moon worship, whether personified as male or female (human gender distinctions are not known to have parallels among angelic beings), have been more deeply embedded in many Middle Eastern cultures (as well as many cultures outside of the Middle East) than we have usually thought. The symbol of the Moon Goddess is the crescent moon. Did the Moon Goddess have anything to do with Diana of the Ephesians? I had seen pictures of the many-breasted statue of Diana numerous times, but it was only during a visit to Turkey that I noticed that her necklace takes the form of the crescent moon! The Moon Goddess has a part in Biblical history. Both Ur of the Chaldeans, where Abraham lived until his father died, were cities ruled over by the Moon Goddess, Sin. Abraham's family worshipped the Moon Goddess, so it would be no exaggeration to suppose that Abraham himself was a convert from the Moon Goddess to Jahweh!" (*Confronting the Queen of Heaven*, C. Peter Wagner, 22-23.) *Baker Theological Dictionary of the Bible* describes The Queen of Heaven as Artemis, who is a Greek goddess. The King James Version calls her Diana. The Israelites faced many different tribes throughout the Bible that worshiped other gods and led them to turn away from the one true God. In the Book of I Kings, chapter 11 tells us that in old age King Solomon did not follow the way of his father, King David, and he turned away his heart from God and began to serve other gods. King Solomon went after Ashtoreth the goddess of the Zidonians, Milcom, the abomination of the ammonites. King Solomon built high places to Chemosh, the abomination of Moab and Molech, the abomination of the children of Ammon, and God was not pleased with King Solomon. These were the new gods that King Solomon's wives were serving, and he joined them when he built altars to serve these strange gods.

What the Kingdom Of Darkness Looks Like and How It Functions

"The principality of darkness manifesting in the forms of the Moon Goddess and Diana of the Ephesians is the Queen of Heaven. One of the names of Diana was "Queen of Heaven." Who is the Queen of Heaven? Quite possibly, the only place in the Bible where God emphatically tells His followers not to pray for certain other people in Jeremiah 7:16. "Do not pray for this people, nor lift up a cry or prayer for them, nor make intercession to Me; for I will not hear you." This is an extraordinary statement reflecting a situation which apparently demands that God's attribute of wrath in this case should overshadow His attribute of mercy. Something really bad must have been happening to provoke such a response. What was it? "(*Confronting the Queen of Heaven*, C. Peter Wagner, 23.)

It involves the Queen of Heaven. The children gather wood, the father kindles the fire, and the women knead their dough to make cakes for the Queen of Heaven (Jeremiah 7:18). Whole families—men, women, and children—are involved in worshipping this unclean territorial spirit of evil. God goes on to say that "they provoke Me to anger."

An even longer passage comes in Jeremiah 44 where the Jews in Egypt were burning incense to her." (Jeremiah 44:17). God pleads, "Oh, do not do this abominable thing that I hate! (Jeremiah 44:4). In fact, it was because the Jews in Jerusalem and Judah had been doing the same thing that God sent them to the 70 years of Babylonian captivity (this is explained in Jeremiah 44:2-3). (*Confronting the Queen of Heaven,* C. Peter Wagner, 23-24.)

In the twenty-first century, we find the same traditions of worshiping false gods continue. When we put sports, hobbies, cars, fishing, finances, resources, and any other thing we worship before God, we have also left our first love. God created us in His image and likeness so that we would truly worship God in spirit and in truth (John 4:23). God created us so we would fully worship Him, and Him alone.

The Great Harlot on Many Waters—"Because God is a God who is not willing that any should perish (see 2 Peter 3:9), my hypothesis is that He hates the Queen of Heaven so much, because she is the demonic principality who is most responsible under Satan for keeping unbelievers in spiritual darkness. It could well be that more people are in Hell today because of the influence of the Queen of Heaven than because of any other spiritual influence. The Queen of Heaven is 'the great harlot who sits on many waters' in Revelation 17. What are the 'waters?' The waters which you saw, where the harlot sits, are peoples, multitudes, nations, and tongues. (Revelation. 17:15). Why have many unreached peoples been impervious to receiving the great blessing that God desires to pour out upon them and upon their nations? Because of the deceptive power of the Queen of Heaven. It is now time to take action! (*Confronting the Queen of Heaven,* Wagner, 24-25.)

In the book of Revelation, the Queen of Heaven is found riding on a scarlet beast and her new name is mystery Babylon, the great, the Mother of Harlots and abominations of the earth. The Queen of Heaven has a very wicked role in deceiving many of the people who are operating in blasphemy, fornication, and every wicked thing that does not please God. Today we have many living in sin; they're fornicating and denying that God exists. While it is yet light, we must work the works that Jesus did before us so that many would be saved from their current lifestyle of living in sin.

The Queen of Heaven takes on other roles in Africa and Asia; she is in charge of ancestor worship. Here is where we see the nations sacrificing their children because the Queen of Heaven is an earth goddess. The Queen of Heaven is also involved with herbalists and witch doctors. The herbalists and witch doctors will be used in the end times against the human race. The Queen of Heaven will work with the Beast to perform healings and miracles. The church must be aware in the end times of how the Kingdom of God operates in signs and wonders, not to be fooled by the lying signs and wonders that will come from the kingdom of darkness.

"Baal is the power that the Canaanites worshipped as god. Baal is the bull god. Baal is in the natural half man and half bull. He is seen in the movies as a Greek Minotaur. Baal is the god of fertility. He was introduced into the world to pollute the spiritual worship of man. Baal was the god that introduced alcoholism, prostitution, tobacco, hallucinatory drugs, sex, murder, and pride to control the victims used through religious worship." (*Mysterious Secrets of the Dark Kingdom*, J.P. Timmons, 115.) In the book of Daniel, Baal was the demon that possessed Nebuchadnezzar when he was suffering insanity. We also see Baal operating in the book of Exodus 32 where the children of Israel worshiped Baal, because they thought Moses was dead when he went up to see God in the Mount. Beelzebub is the Lord of the Flies who controls all things that fly. Beelzebub is responsible for the witches and wizards that fly in the night to the spirit world. Beelzebub is in charge of the blood sacrifices made to Satan. The blood sacrifices are where the witch or wizard kills a human being, drains their blood and gives it to Satan who drinks human blood. Beelzebub is also responsible for the destruction and loss of life.

In the Book of 1 Kings 16:32-33, King Ahab ruled after the death of his father Omri. King Ahab married Jezebel, the daughter of King Ethbaal who was King of the Zidonians. King Solomon also served the god of the Zidonians. King Ahab went to serve Baal and worship the Zidonians' god. It was Elijah who destroyed the worship of Baal by killing the 450 prophets of Baal and the 400 prophets of the grove. The Israelites left God to serve a stone god and when the stone god could not bring fire to burn up the sacrifice, and after Elijah laid wood, stones, and dust and filled moats around the altar with water and set it all afire to be destroyed by God, did they return to serve the Lord, and cried that He is God.

"Ariton is responsible for all the demons involved with magical powers. Ariton deals with charms that provide people with power in the physical world. The charms allow people to gain power, sex, and money. Charms can be used to allow people to become millionaires and to kill their enemies. Mirrors are also used by Ariton to kill people; the mirrors are used to summon people up. If you appear in the mirror, then you'll be killed. If you turn your back to the mirror when they summon your spirit, you live; they have no power over the mirror and your spirit." (*Mysterious Secrets of the Dark Kingdom*, J.P. Timmons, 117.)

In the Book of Acts 8:9 -24, we see that Simon was a sorcerer who bewitched the people of Samaria. When Peter and John came down to Samaria to assist Phillip in laying on of hands to the Samarians to receive the Baptism of the Holy Spirit, the people received. Simon wanted to purchase the power that Peter and John displayed. Peter told Simon that his heart was not right with God.

Mammon is the demon over money. Mammon is the god that possesses mankind through the love of money. Mammon is responsible for establishing contracts involving money and its distribution. The wealthy families are located throughout the world. The money the wealthy families used are to support war, politics, and distribution of drugs. The Bible states in 1 Timothy that the "love of money is the root of all evil." When Christians who are tithing are struggling and they have a big heart to give into the Kingdom of God, know that Mammon is at work against your finances. Mammon's job is to stop the Christians from giving into the Kingdom of God. Mammon is the responsible demon for poverty and financial destruction." (*Mysterious Secrets of The Kingdom of Darkness*, J.P. Timmons, 119.)

Money used in the Old Testament reflects how Joseph was sold into slavery by his brothers for twenty shekels (Genesis 37:28). In the New Testament, Jesus was betrayed by Judas who sold him to the High Priest for thirty pieces of silver (Zacharias. 11:13; Mark 14:11; Luke 22:5).

We see today that many people hold tight to their money (Malachi 3:8-10). We rob God in the church today by not bringing in our tithes and offerings by giving 10 percent of what we earn back to God. We see the rich in the world robbing the poor and those who are in the kingdom must compensate to ensure that we have the compassion of Christ and feed those who are in need. Ananias and Sapphira died for lying to the Holy Spirit and trying to rob God (Acts 5: 1-10).

"Paimon is the demon responsible for crystals. Paimon works with people by speaking through mirrors, crystal balls, and water. Paimon is the demon responsible to operate through familiar spirits. Paimon is also responsible to fool people as if he is the voice of God. Paimon is the counterfeit to the Gifts of the Holy Spirit. Asmodee is the demon involved with sexual immorality; he marries people for Satan. Asmodee is responsible for the spirit of Jezebel in the Bible who works with Baal in 1 Kings 16:30-33. When we see pastors falling into sexual immorality, homosexuality, adultery, and marital conflict, we see people who are being attacked. Asmodee is primarily responsible for perversion, pornography, and prostitution." (*Mysterious Secrets of the Dark Kingdom*, J.P. Timmons, 122,125.)

Today, we see that the sex slave trade (which we now call human trafficking), abduction of children, teens, youth, and women or men to serve our polluted sex drives and destroy innocent lives. The spirit of perversion, pornography, and prostitution has driven human beings who are stable to fall in their personal lives. We see destroyed families because of the distorted lifestyles that either the husband or wife chose. When we choose to embrace the lies of the enemy, we are not hearing the voice of God. "My sheep hear my voice and the voice of a stranger it will not follow."

"Magog is the demon of war. Magog teaches people and nations to make war. Magog's ultimate assignment is to wage war no matter who wins. Magog uses other demons, white witches, and humans to develop new machinery and technology of weaponry to wage war and kill. Magog uses anger and hate to stir up war between people and nations." (*Mysterious Secrets of the Dark Kingdom*, J.P. Timmons, 127.) We can see this demon evident in the Islamic nations where they kill people who are not Muslim in Islamic nations around the world. We witness the demons operating in the ethnic cleansing of nations at war such as Somali, Rwanda, Nigeria, Sudan, and the Civil War in Kenya.

What the Kingdom Of Light Looks Like and How It Functions

When the Kingdom of God operates, there is love, hope, peace, joy, happiness, meekness, grace, long suffering, gentleness, kindness, goodness, humbleness, boldness, self-esteem, self-control, and temperance. We don't see God's kingdom operating in trying to kill children. In God's kingdom, we are preserving life, not taking life. God's kingdom is built on love, not war. We see the Kingdom of God defending not sacrificing human life and killing it to get blood to sacrifice to Satan. God is the author of life. We see fellowship and true signs and wonders in God's kingdom. We bring our tithes and offering to build, not tear down the Kingdom of God. In God's kingdom people, marriage consists of one man and one woman. We are not married to two men or two women in God's kingdom. We don't worship idols in God's kingdom. We don't worship mammon in God's kingdom, but we worship God. We have fellowship and relationship with God. We have no other gods but God whom we serve. In God's kingdom we are not angry or hateful to, or jealous or envious of others. In God's kingdom we don't tell lies, we don't steal, and we don't kill our enemies.

Matthew 5:5 says, "Blessed are the poor in spirit for theirs is the kingdom of heaven." Matthew 5:4: "Blessed are they that mourn for they shall be comforted." Matthew 5:6: "Blessed are the meek, for they shall inherit the earth." Matthew 5:7: "Blessed are they which hunger and thirst after righteousness for they shall be filled." Matthew 5:8: "Blessed are the pure in heart, for they shall see God." Matthew 5:9: "Blessed are the peacemakers, for they shall be called the children of God." Matthew 5:10: "Blessed are they which are persecuted for righteousness sake, for theirs is the kingdom of heaven." Matthew 5:11: "Blessed are ye, when men shall revile you, and persecute you, and shall say all manner of evil against you falsely, for my sake." Matthew 5:14: "Ye are the light of the world. A city that is set on a hill cannot be hid. Matthew 5:16: "Let your light so shine before men, that they may see your good works, and glorify your Father which is in heaven."

The Kingdom of God is about the light shining in a dark place to bring truth where there has been no truth. God's kingdom sheds light where lies and deception, deceit, despair, doubt, and discouragement abounds. God's kingdom is not the author of confusion or rebellion, which is as witchcraft. God's kingdom operates in honoring rather than dishonoring. God's kingdom is not jealous or envious, but operates in esteeming others higher than ourselves. When we see the Kingdom of God in its full operation, we see it operate in the opposite spirit of the kingdom of darkness. Darkness exists because of the sinful acts that men and women have chosen freely by their own will. Darkness can flee when we make a conscious decision to live by the kingdom of light.

Chapter Three
Demons in the Bible

The demons described in Chapter Two of the Two Kingdoms are the demons we will discuss further in this chapter. The four main principalities that serve Satan are Apollyon, Abaddon, Belial, and the Beast number 666. These four main principalities have eight powers working with them. The eight powers are called Ashtaroth, Baal, Magog, Beelzebub, Asmodee, Mammon, Paimon, and Ariton.

How the Demons in the Bible Serve the Kingdom of Darkness

The demons that are working in the earth today travel from the second heaven and work on earth through human beings who are serving Satan. Their work system is much like ours. If you were working for a civilian company and you did good work, you would be promoted, or incentives would be provided to you to keep helping the company go forth; so it is with the demons. A private corporation advances, and then you also will advance. Promotion comes for them when they do something that allows the kingdom of darkness to advance. The incentives are offered to keep one going and in bondage to Satan.

"Apollyon's main function is to turn people away from God into idolatry and into false religions. Abaddon is the polluting demon. He is responsible for corrupting habits, such as smoking cigarettes, using cocaine and other drugs, listening to rock music, delving into pornography, homosexuality, fornication, incest, bestiality, pedophilia, and alcohol. Belial's main function is to cause war and death. Belial likes to destroy people and see them die. The Beast is Satan's end time demon. He is responsible for wide-scale destruction and desolation for the human race. The Beast can transform himself into 666 different forms." (*Mysterious Secrets of the Dark kingdom*, J.P. Timmons, 101.)

In *Baker Theological Dictionary of the Bible*, we see John's vision of the fifth trumpet blowing (Revelation 9:1-11) and demonic horsemen are seen coming out of an open abyss. When these demonic horsemen are released, they begin to torment those who are still on earth during the great tribulation. The torment is described to be so great but no one is killed during the demonic tormenting. Abaddon is the Greek name given for Apollyon. Apollyon is the Hebrew name given for the demons destroying and bringing destruction to human lives on the earth.

During a visit to the Carolinas, we were asked to provide support in taking back the region. The region had been infiltrated by principalities, powers, and rulers of darkness. A thriving resort industry that was booming and making money for the Kingdom of God was now going under in resources, devastation, and destruction that loomed over the business and the families in the region. When we visited the property, you could feel and see in the spirit that the area had been hit drastically. When you are on an assignment like this, you must ensure that all the members on the team are in unity and that egos are checked at the door. The enemy will look for a crack in the wall to see if he can cause disaster among the team you take to assist if you are not united. God will prepare you and warn you in advance what you will encounter before it occurs. God will also confirm how he will assist you when they turn against you in the midst of the battle.

The first step was to identify what had come into the territory and why it was allowed to come in. We identified the problem: death and destruction had been assigned. We went case by case taking back the territory and breaking the powers of death and destruction over the region. The success of taking back the region came with a heavy price. The backlash caused God to place me in a protective spiritual bubble so that I could not be destroyed from within the team. When intense spiritual warfare takes place between the kingdom of darkness and the kingdom of light, expect casualties. The casualty that resulted was a broken relationship with the team at the end. The price was small to pay to liberate an entire region of families and businesses. Our goal was to complete the mission for the Kingdom of God. We were successful in reestablishing the Kingdom of God and pushing the kingdom of darkness out of the territory. We watched as the attempt to cause people to lose their lives stopped, and business experienced instant recovery.

The Spirits That Fall Under Each Demon As Identified In the Bible

The powers serving the principalities' functions are to support the top four demons of Satan. "Ashtaroth's main function is to operate as a goddess called the Queen of Heaven. Ashtaroth is in charge of nature religions and promotes false religions. Ashtaroth is goddess of fertility, harvest worship and satanic healings, occultism, astrology, divination, and fortune telling. Baal is the god of fertility. Baal is responsible for murder, pride, drugs, tobacco, and sexual immorality. Beelzebub is responsible for collecting the blood sacrifices made to Satan. Beelzebub oversees everything that flies in the spirit realm, including witches and wizards that fly from earth to second heaven. Beelzebub feeds on human blood once the humans are killed. Ariton is responsible for all magical powers. Ariton operates from charms and mirrors to promote people through sex, power, and money. Mammon is responsible for the storehouse of Satan. Mammon sells charms, spirits, magic mirrors, and fame. Mammon is assigned to keep money out of the hands of the Christians. Paimon is responsible for the crystals. Paimon pretends to be the voice of God. Paimon is the counterfeit to the Gifts of the Holy Spirit.

Paimon operates as an angel of light like Satan." (*Mysterious Secrets of the Kingdom of Darkness,* J.P. Timmons, 110.)

Ashtaroth was found in the book of Samuel (1 Samuel 3:6-10). The Israelites encounter this goddess during their settling in the land of Canaan. Eli, Samuel, and King Saul had direct confrontations with this demon goddess. It took Josiah, an eight-year-old boy, who became King over Israel, to clean the house of God by destroying the shrines that were erected by Solomon. Josiah made it clear that there was only one true God and that was Yahweh. Baal was the god under whom Israel fell in numerous incidents in the book of Judges. In the book of 1 Kings 16:29-34, King Ahab and Jezebel declared that Israel would worship Baal as the national deity. Priests offered sacrifices of animals to the god Baal, and depending on where they were located, the leaders offered their sons to Baal by fire. In Mark 3:22, Jesus was considered by the scribes to be called Beelzebub because he cast devils out of people. Ariton is found in the spirit of divination which the Apostle Paul encountered in the Book of Acts 16:16-35, when a slave girl who was possessed with the spirit of divination, and by grieving the spirit in Apostle Paul, he cast that spirit out of her. Mammon is described in *Baker Theological Dictionary of the Bible* as an Aramaic word meaning money, wealth, or property (Matthew 6:24). The use of wealth is discussed in the Bible 2,400 times. Jesus knew that mankind would have issues of wealth. When we place security in money and not in the Lord Jesus Christ, we will fall to the schemes of the enemy. In the New Testament Scriptures, Ananias and Sapphira lost their lives for lying about the cost of property to the Holy Spirit. Paimon in the Book of Samuel (1 Samuel 3:1-21) is an example of how Samuel learned how to hear the voice of God. When we hear the true voice of God, we cannot be deceived by Paimon who pretends to be the voice of God. God spoke to Samuel when he was in the temple. Eli taught Samuel what to say when the Lord spoke to him. The Word of God also states that "My sheep hear My voice." We will be able to hear the voice of the Lord when we have developed a relationship close to God so that the voice of the enemy will not trap you to trip and fall to Satan's voice.

"Asmodee is responsible for sexual immorality. Asmodee functions in prostitution, sexual perversion, homosexuality, lesbianism, bestiality, and barrenness of the womb. Contempt, in marriage and marital conflict, repeated divorces, inability to form relationships in marriages, miscarriages, and death of children. Magog is responsible for war. Magog is responsible for the demons over anger, fear, and hate that cause war. Magog operates out of the demon spirit of unforgiveness." (*Mysterious Secrets of the Dark Kingdom*, J.P. Timmons, 124-127.)

With Asmodee in the book of Matthew 5:31-32; 19: 8-9, we see where prostitution and adultery were discussed based on illicit sexual conduct. Today, we find that fornication is running rampant in the world. We find married couples swapping husbands and wives and having orgies as they did in the Roman Empire. We find that if we study history, the things that are going on in the world today and in the church are happening to those who are lukewarm. We find this in the book of Revelation 2:14, 21 where sin and fornication abound in the church. Revelation 3:15-16 says that if the people are lukewarm, God will spit them out of his mouth. The church is doing the very same sins that the world is doing when dealing with the same sexually immoral issues in families today. In the book of Isaiah 54, the barren woman was not able to have children. We can also look at Hannah and Rachel, whose wombs were closed until the Lord opened them to allow them to have children. When Abraham lied about Sarah being his sister and gave her to Abimelech, his entire household became barren of having children (Genesis 20:17). Magog, in the book of Exodus 17:8-16, Moses and the Israelites fought the Amalekites. The Amalekites had attacked the Israelites' rear and were killing them. Moses defeated the Amalekites when Aaron and Hur held up his hands to win the war. God wanted the Amalekites eliminated so they could not harm Israel.

Chapter Four
Root Causes

Root causes are the areas of our lives where we allowed the enemy to continue to hold us in bondage. Root causes are areas that cannot be seen in life but eventually will spring up when least expected.

How Root Causes of the Spirit Operate

Root causes manifest through sickness, fear, unforgiveness, resentment, bitterness, rebellion, anxiety, stress, pride, poor self-image, rejection, abandonment, shame, guilt, self-hatred, self-rejection, jealousy, anger, rage, violence, murder, guilt, suicide, perfection, dumb and deaf spirit, worry, depression, oppression, self-condemnation, trauma, allergies, addiction, false burdens, identity, confusion, abortion, lack of love, perfectionism, manipulation, and control. The list provides you with some examples of what root causes are. If you are experiencing some of these root causes, you might see if you left a door open for the enemy to attack you legally. You want to ensure that all doors are closed to the enemy.

"The Bible usually states the devil has a host of fallen angelic followers who are ready and eager in their efforts to hurt man and defeat God's kingdom on earth." (*Guide to Spiritual Warfare,* E.M. Bounds, 14.)

How Access Doors Are Given To the Spirits

In this section, you will learn how access doors are given to evil spirits. When we willfully sin, we provide legal ground to the enemy to come in and attack our families and us. As we look through the sixty-six books in the Old and New Testaments, we see how sin ran all through the Bible. Today, we see that sin is still the access door that allows the enemy to torment and hinder us from moving in God's kingdom. In order to close the access door, we need to ask God for forgiveness of our sins and repent for the sin we committed. Once the sin is placed under the blood of Jesus, then Satan and the demons that torment the body of Christ and our families no longer has access.

Legal ground (2 Corinthians 4:2) (disobedience) is a term used in deliverance when the enemy has a right to attack you because you have doors open (Genesis 4:7) that allow him to come back and attack you legally. The term we used is called the legal ground given by willfully committing sin (Ephesians 2:2-3). The way to keep the door shut is to walk in love at all times. Christians must learn to release people (Galatians 5:1) even when they have been hurt by someone who is close to them, whether it is a friend or a family member. Remember, the enemy has had over 5,000 years to study our families. He knows what it takes to get us angry and fighting. He is the author of confusion that keeps trouble stirred up.

The second term is called blind intrusion (innocent). The enemy comes to attack you even if you have no sin. The blind intrusion is that you are living in unity (Psalm 133:1-6); you are seeing things eye to eye. The family has no arguments, and everyone is getting along well with one another. You will find out that, whether you have opened a door or not, the enemy will still attack you (Job 2:3-7). The blind intrusion door is the door that the Lord will protect because you are righteous (Deuteronomy 6:8) and have been living as a disciple of God. We must ensure that we are walking and living the model of Jesus here on earth and are living examples of the Kingdom of God.

The Five Access Doors

There are five access doors (Genesis 4:7) we give to the enemy. The first access door is called unforgiveness. Let's take a look at unforgiveness. Unforgiveness plays a major role in root causes that leads to deliverance. Many people today are harboring unforgiveness in their hearts against one another. If someone hurts you through rape, molestation, or incest, we must be willing to forgive them. We find that people today are sick and suffering due to unforgiveness. People are refusing to forgive the person who hurt them. Unforgiveness leads to bitterness if you fail to forgive and release the person who hurt you. Many are walking around with illnesses and diseases all because they refuse to forgive and release the person who committed the infraction against them. In the book of Matthew 5:23-24, the Bible describes the story of a person having unforgiveness with his brother and the person wants a gift to be accepted by God. In order for the gift to be accepted by God, the person must return to the family member and ask for forgiveness. Then that person is allowed to go back and take his gift to the altar and God will receive the gift from the person, because they have forgiven their brother.

The second access door is bitterness. Bitterness comes from unforgiveness and if a person is going to break the power of bitterness, he must first forgive. Bitterness also results from the heart of a person turning away from God. Hardness of heart results in bitterness toward God when facing many misfortunes in life. When we hold grudges against people and are not willing to release them, we have hardened our hearts. An example of a hardened heart in Old Testament Scripture is Pharaoh in Egypt. He hardened his heart against God and would not allow the Israelites to leave Egypt. It provided an access door for sickness to enter Pharaoh. The quicker we forgive our enemies, the sooner doors close to bitterness.

The third access door is resentment. Resentment comes when people have been rejected and abandoned. We find resentment plays a major role when an authority figure treats a person unjustly. When resentment transpires in life, we still have to learn to forgive the people who rejected or abandoned us. How a person was raised in life will determine how they treat the next generation. If one generation was treated badly, it has an opportunity to change the behavior pattern or to pass it down to the next generation. People must learn that the quicker they release those who have harmed them, the sooner they can walk freely in their hearts. If resentment is carried too long, it will incapacitate a person from moving forward to the call and destiny in life.

The fourth access door is trauma. Trauma will immobilize a person if they stay stuck in the traumatic experience that occurred in their life, even if there is a requirement for deep inner healing of the memory picture that the enemy continues to play from that past. A person who has been traumatized must also forgive and release the people who tried to hurt them. Inner healing is deliverance for traumatized people. It provides the Holy Spirit an avenue in which to confront the memories. It allows the Holy Spirit an opportunity to press out the wounds until the person is fully whole and functioning in life again, despite the past.

The fifth and final access door is called vows (swear) (Matthew 5:33-37). We must be careful when we make vows. Many people today are stuck because of the spoken vows they made when they were young. An example of a vow would be if a person was married and made a statement, such as, "I'll never love that person again." Here is an example of a person making a vow. If a person was wounded by an authority figure, and they made a vow of never trusting authority figures again, that is a vow. When we make vows, we need to ensure that we repent for the vows we made and ask God to forgive us. When the door is shut, the enemy no longer has a right to defeat us because of the vows we made.

How to Combat the Spirits

Matthew 18:18: "Verily I say unto you, whatsoever ye shall bind on earth shall be bound in heaven: and whatsoever ye shall loose on earth shall be loosed in heaven." Webster's dictionary defines the word 'bind' as "to make secure by trying: to confine, restrain, or restrict as if with bonds: to constrain with legal authority: to exert a restraining or compelling effect." Other definitions include: to arrest, apprehend, handcuff, lead captive, take charge of, and lock up. To fetter, manacle, shackle, chain. To restrain, hold back, check, curb, put a brake on, call a halt, and put a stop to. Binding is done by legal authority. We have legal authority in the name of Jesus to bind the works of darkness. The works of darkness encompass sin, iniquity, perversion, sickness, disease, infirmity, death, destruction, curses, witchcraft, sorcery, divination, poverty, lack, divorce, strife, lust, pride, rebellion, fear, torment, and confusion.

"We have legal authority to put a stop to these things in our lives and in the lives of those we minister to." Loose means to untie, to free from restraint, and to detach. It also means to disjoin, divorce, separate, unhitch, get free, get loose, escape, break away, unbind, unchain, unfetter, free, release, unlock, liberate, disconnect, and forgive.

People need to be loosed from bloodline curses, evil inheritance, familiar spirits, sin, guilt, shame, condemnation, control, domination and manipulation from other people, mind control, religious control, sickness, disease, deception, false teaching, sin, habits, worldliness, carnality, flesh, demons, tradition, ungodly soul ties, ungodly oaths, pledges, vows, spoken curses, hexes, vex, jinxes, past experiences of trauma and cults. We have legal authority, in the name of Jesus, to loose ourselves and others we minister to from the results of sin. (*Deliverance & Spiritual Warfare Manual*, John Eckhart, 7-8.) We have been given the tools and the keys to the Kingdom of God to help others who are caught in captivity to be set free from the spirits that bind them.

Interview Results with Pastors and Ministers

Deliverance in North American Churches—Demonic oppression has largely been ignored in North American churches. As to unbelievers, this is partly due to the conviction of many that belief in demons is mere superstition, and partly because unbelievers are not likely to seek deliverance help or to be accepted for such ministry if they do seek help. The church has also largely ignored demonic oppression among its members, partly due to the theology of some that a true believer cannot be oppressed by demonic spirits and that therefore all evil spirits leave a new believer at the time of his conversion, and partly due to the noisy, unpleasant, and often humiliating method of deliverance common until recent years. The long-standing indifference of the western church to demonic oppression or "demonization" is changing. The theology that a demon cannot reside in a true believer is giving way as a result of teaching and experience. (*Ministry Training Manual Clark,* Randy M-2-M-3.)

The following questions were asked to pastors and ministers who have administered deliverance.

- **As pastors and leaders who administer deliverance ministry, why is it that churches do not perform deliverance ministries in their churches?**

Pastor Dan Hammer states, "I think that many have not been trained or feel uncomfortable dealing with demons from my experience."

Pastor Doug Martin states, "There are a number of reasons why deliverance ministries are not performed in some churches. In some cases, it's because of theological belief. They do not believe that deliverance is a ministry that is valid for today. In some cases, it is due to unbelief, just as Jesus said in Matthew 13:58 that He could not do many miracles there because of their lack of faith. Another factor is lack of understanding about demonic powers and deliverance. If they don't know what they're dealing with and/or how to deal with it, then they will choose to do nothing. In some cases, it may be due to 'not wanting to create a scene,' since sometimes deliverance can attract a lot of attention. Lastly, belief over deliverance in churches varies and it may be avoided in order to not create controversy or disunity."

Pastor Scott Smith states, "Fear of the unknown. Limited expectations from 'Ministry Schools.' Fear of failure. It is not considered 'safe.' Unwilling to pay the price—holiness, prayer, fasting, and focused Word study. Don't want to end up doing it all themselves, because it may be hard to find trustworthy people.

Minister Sue Thomson and Minister Anita Young state, "I think that sometimes deliverance ministry is seen as controversial. And being respectable is too important and fear of what deliverance will look like. Also maybe churches misunderstand the authority all Christians have to cast out demons. Some Christians don't believe a Christian can have a demon." Minister Kari Zevenbergen states, "In what I have experienced, it is the administration or the lead pastor who lacks the correct teachings or understanding of deliverance. Also some of them do not obtain the gifts of deliverance so they will not allow it to be in the church."

- **What would you say is different in deliverance ministries today than in the past twenty-five years?**

Pastor Dan Hammer states, "People have been better equipped to minister deliverance. There are many more books and teachings on deliverance. There are also many training services as well. All of these have helped more Christians to be equipped to minister deliverance with the Lord's direction.

Pastor Doug Martin states, "Although there are still those who do not believe in deliverance today, there is much more openness to the supernatural today. Thus, people are more willing to at least consider the possibility of demonic existence and influence in a person's life. Over the last twenty-five years, much has been written about and taught from various sources about deliverance. In general, this has given a better understanding about demonic powers and deliverance so that deliverance has been done with more success than in the past."

Pastor Scott Smith states, "Twenty-five years ago, few dared to engage; a few prayer warriors who knew the Word, and who were in Christ. It was manifestation initiated. Now there are valuable teaching resources produced by a generation of practitioners. Seminars, practical training workshops, books, and organized deliverance ministry groups like I.S.D.M. The great need is forcing us to facilitate equipping and accountability."

Minister Sue Thomson and Minister Anita Young state, "There is more good training today than twenty-five years ago. And I think today the body of Christ has more of a vision for Isaiah 61 being fulfilled, which includes deliverance. I also see the body of Christ accepting the fact that Christians can have a demon and can be oppressed by the demonic realm."

Minister Kari Zevenbergen states, "In the past, deliverance, I believe, happened outside the church with tents, crusades, revivals, or outside on the streets and within homes. Today, it happens quietly and is pushed in a room so people can't see. In other continents, yes, you will see vast huge corporate deliverance because the roof of control is not in effect."

- **How many successful cases have you had in deliverance?**

Pastor Dan Hammer: "Over the years, I've been involved with hundreds."

Pastor Doug Martin: "Much of the ministry I do does not involve deliverance ministry, but I would estimate that I have been involved with about twenty-five different situations where I was involved in deliverance counseling/prayer. Of those, I would say I have seen definite results in about half of those situations."

Pastor Scott Smith: "Approximately 200 'walking it out' is sometimes impossible to track, such as missions trips, evangelism, etc.

Minister Sue Thomson and Minister Anita Young: "Approximately 180 total."

Minister Kari Zevenbergen: "Approximately 1,000 total."

Survey of People Who Have Been Delivered

The following questions were asked to individuals receiving deliverance. Names will not be released in the results to provide confidentiality for those who received the ministry of deliverance.

- **How did you feel when you first went through your deliverance session?**

Survey 1: "Apprehension and scared due to not knowing what to expect. I didn't know what I was getting myself into. Embarrassed of what I had revealed. Feeling naked and exposed at first, then as we were going through the deliverance, I became more comfortable. I was made to feel that I had nothing to be afraid of or embarrassed about. I was surprised at what was deep inside of me. I didn't know a pain was deep and hidden even from me."

Survey 2: "Before the session, I was as low, despondent, conflicted, troubled, and oppressed as I had ever been in my life. After the session, I had the sense that I had been 'cleansed,' or cleared the spiritual slate and felt like it was a new beginning. I felt encouraged, uplifted, strengthened, etc. My sense of depression or oppression seemed 'lifted,' and I didn't feel the pressure of being overwhelmed by everything in life. That place of defeat being attacked from every angle in life had been overcome and I felt victorious. That lasted several months, even one and a half years."

Survey 3: "Hopeless, uniformed; knew of God but didn't know him; didn't realize what I was doing or saying to people or how I hurt them."

Survey 4: "Excited and a little doubtful. Deliverance was a very new concept to me. I also had high hopes and expectations, but nothing happened the way I thought it would. I didn't really 'notice' a change. I just claimed afterward in faith, 'I've been delivered.'"

Survey 5: "I didn't know what to expect as I had never heard of the deliverance process through the church. In my spirit, I could feel that the Lord was getting ready to do surgery on me. My heart began to swell up with tears. We dealt with many deep rooted issues of generational sin (freemasonry), lust, murder, hatred, and unforgiveness. After many hours of repenting and renouncing demonic curses, I felt like a huge weight was lifted off of me. I was exhausted but after four-and-a-half hours, I felt a freedom like I had never experienced before."

- **Have you fallen back since you were delivered?**

Survey 1: "No, I really wasn't dealing with any major outward sins. It was more a deliverance from any hindrance from my past, the emotional part."

Survey 2: "After several months, 12-14 periods of sustained victory, obedience, and productivity, I experienced a return of the torment from cravings to use cocaine again and pornography as well. Unfortunately, I succumbed to the fantasies and went back into sin. I had become lazy about staying in the Word. My prayer life was horrible. I didn't do a good job of taking thoughts into captivity in the time period leading up to finally acting on my desire."

Survey 3: "As you and Scott were doing deliverance, it was like you knew my personal thoughts, feelings, and past that only I knew. I didn't know how easy it would be to follow the Lord. I done it [sic] and I love you for helping me."

Survey 4: "In a few areas, a few times I've confessed and renounced and thanked Him that He is faithful and just to forgive when I confess."

Survey 5: "Yes, I did fall back into sin of lust for an old boyfriend. It was difficult to let go of these memories as I didn't know how to replace them with new memories. I struggled with how to love my dad and mom when I went home to visit them. The Masonic spirit is so dark and strong in their house, it was difficult to love them. Changing my thought patterns was the most difficult part of turning my heart around."

- **Are you successfully walking out your deliverance?**

Survey 1: "I believe so."

Survey 2: "At this moment two year later, after having slipped twice back into my former pattern of bi-polar, inconsistent Christianity of being hot and cold, in and out, up and down, I now am walking with the Lord like never before. I became immersed in the Word about six months ago. The truth in the Word as it relates to the cross and what the gospel really is has become alive and real to me. I am recognizing several things that the absolute 'reality' is that I have been buried in the likeness of His death. When He died, I died and I died to sin. Plus all of my sins past, present, and future were really buried in the tomb with Him. And when He rose, I actually truly rose with Him to walk in newness of life. I am a new creature despite what the enemy tells me or what the circumstances 'seem' like. Knowing that truth and truly believing it has caused me to walk it out in victory and power. I now realize from the Word, that Christ's death on the cross and His shed blood was the victory. That's when the debt was paid in full. Every gift the believer has comes through that power, victory, discernment, wisdom, and abundant life; healing is mine. As long as I daily keep taking up my cross, denying myself, and following Him, I will make the cross the object exclusively of my faith and allow the Holy Spirit the opportunity to execute the power.

Survey 3: "Yes, still fall, but I get right back up and keep on going."

Survey 4: "I say yes, by God's grace. Sue and Anita are coming over to my place tomorrow to pray, because there has been a harassing spirit or something that keeps turning up. So having done all, I stand."

Survey 5: "Yes, today I can say that I am! It took many months of turning towards the Lord and allowing Him to change my thoughts. I started spending more time in His Word and at the altar praying, fasting, and worshipping Him. I think the key to this success is surrounding yourself with like-minded believers who want to see you succeed in your walk with the Lord. I am in a healthy church where the atmosphere is to see sinners redeemed and restored. Also, the Lord began to fill my heart with compassion and mercy. Those two ingredients were keys to me being able to love my enemies."

Statistics

The pastors and ministers were asked to rate the success of their deliverance ministries. The following are the results provided from the leaders' ratings.

On a scale of 1-5 (1 being lowest, and 5 being highest), how would you rate the cases in deliverance ministries from members of your church in how effective the deliverance sessions were?

	1	2	3	4	5

Pastor 1: 4.5

Pastor 2: 3

Pastor 3: 3-5

Minister 4: 5

Minister 5: 3

Overall average 3.5 = effectiveness in deliverance.

Pastor Dan Hammer states, "I would rate our church 4.5 in effectiveness. We deal with deliverance on a regular basis."

Pastor Doug Martin states, "On an average, I would say that the deliverances I have seen or been a part of in our church would rate about 3 in effectiveness.

Pastor Scott Smith states, "There are two cases that were much more complicated than just deliverance; extreme health complications. Extreme inner healing still needed. Maybe 3 for more healing needed. Most are probably 4. Few 5s where total transformation was more immediate. I am happy with the effectiveness even though we all press toward the 'one' touch."

Minister Sue Thomson and Minister Anita Young state, "Rate a 5."

Minister Kari Zevenbergen states, "Scale deliverance in the church is 3 with surface healing taking place in churches. Need the roots and deep deliverance to take place in people's lives.

On a scale of 1-5 (1 being lowest and 5 being highest), how would you rate the cases in deliverance ministries from people coming from other denominations that you performed deliverance and how effective were the deliverance sessions?

	1	2	3	4	5

Pastor 1: 4.5

Pastor 2: 2

Pastor 3: 3-5

Minister4: 2

Minister 5: 5

Overall average 3.5 = effectiveness in deliverance for other denominations

Pastor Dan Hammer states, "I would rate our church 4.5 in this category. Different churches send people to us for deliverance."

Pastor Doug Martin states, "I would rate deliverances from people from other churches or denominations at a 2. Some of the reasons being those mentioned in question 1. They are skeptical about deliverance ministry due to theological beliefs, lack of understanding, or experience with deliverance. There is not a trusting relationship between me and the individual, because we don't know each other, so they may be hesitant to share their needs and life experiences with me. This aspect affects the ability to evaluate what type of ministry they need.

Pastor Scott Smith states, "There are many times very desperate people who are willing to risk whatever they have to for help. They are very cooperative and transparent, which usually gives an excellent result. I would rate them usually between a scales of 3-5 based on their honesty. Many have ended up coming to our church with family and friends that need help.

Minister Sue Thomson and Minister Anita Young state, "Rate a 2."

Minister Kari Zevenbergen states, "In the church, a rate of 2; outside the church, a rate of 5. It's harder to perform deliverance on church people. People who have not been in church are easier. The roof of church is how effective the spirit of God can be effective to do deliverance. If the authority of the head is not in agreement with deliverance, you can only perform the level on which they allow. Administration and leaders will either hinder the process of deliverance or let the freedom of deliverance rise to the people. Different levels for different churches."

The individuals surveyed were asked to rate the expectation and success of the deliverance sessions from the deliverance ministries. The following are the results of the ratings provided from the individuals surveyed.

On a scale of 1-5 (1 being lowest and 5 being highest), how would you rate your session in deliverance? Did it fulfill your expectations or not?

1   2   3   4   5

Survey 1: 5

Survey 2: 5

Survey 3: 5

Survey 4: 5

Survey 4: 5

Overall average 5 = expectations in deliverance

Survey 1: "Only because we didn't get to finish the last part. It had gone a long time and we were going to get back together to finish the freemasonry part, but other than that, a 5."

Survey 2: "Because I was down so low and really did pull out of it. Scott and Penny spent 5-6 hours with me. Above and beyond the call of duty, and really did an in depth, exhaustive procedure. 5+."

Survey 3: "5 plus; you opened my eyes, heart, and soul. Thank you."

Survey 4: "It didn't 'fulfill' my expectations, because my expectations were so radically different from what actually happened, but Sue and Anita had prepared me ahead of time that would probably be the case. So I'd say a 5 out of 5 because it was effective and just what God wanted it to be!"

Survey 5: "I would rate it as a 5. Both Penny and Pastor Scott were very skilled and prepared to deal with the demonic realm. They knew how to pray through these issues. I believe that God uses humble people who are filled with a tremendous amount of mercy and grace. Both of them have a love to see souls restored and healed. They were both wonderful to work with. I always thought it was funny that God would use a "Giant" (Pastor Scott) and a "General" (Penny) to help me fight this spiritual battle. I guess He knew I needed the best soldiers in His army."

On a scale of 1-5 (1 being the lowest, 5 the highest), how would you rate your deliverance session? Was it successful or not?

1	2	3	4	5

Survey 1: 5

Survey 2: 5

Survey 3: 5

Survey 4: 5

Survey 5: 4

Overall average 5 = successful in deliverance

Survey 1: "As stated on question 4, we didn't get finished so I think it is a work in progress. Otherwise 5 seeing that I had already been through years of counseling and nothing had ever touched that deep inside of me before. It really surprised me, so on that level I would say a 5. I don't know if the remainder of the session would matter, but otherwise I was very pleased that I went through it."

Survey 2: "Yes, for a time, but I learned eventually that in order to start having a consistent walk that I need to take off the spiritual 'training wheels' and get off the milk, and get in the Word myself. I know if I did that I could be fully equipped for every good work and walk worthy of the calling."

Survey 3: "Penny, I would rate you a 10. You're an awesome person of God and I am happy you're in my life. You helped me get my life back. The enemy knew I would fall, but you were there to help me get back up. Penny, you are an awesome person. I thank you for helping me get right with God. Love you and God Bless you. I would rate a 5."

Survey 4: "I say yes, 5 out of 5. I'm walking out my freedom and there is probably now a deeper level of healing needed, but the deliverance freed me up to get to this place. Thank you for this ministry."

Survey 5: "I would rate it a 4. I had been trapped in a mental prison for over thirty years. I thought I was a good Christian woman, but

I couldn't understand why I was so unhappy and mad at the world all the time. I was bound in chains with a fragmented heart, and I believe that this deliverance session helped me to put the pieces back together; restoring me back to wholeness. The only suggestion I would have is that at the end of the deliverance session, I wish I had more tools to help me turn and change my mindset. Meaning, if there were a set of guidelines to help me turn from my old way of thinking (prayer, intercession, serving, reading His Word, forgiveness, accountability etc., then I may not have fallen back into my old sinful nature. Also, I was very fortunate that I allowed myself to be accountable to a sister at church. Weekly, we checked in with each other, and she lifted me up when I was weak. Overall, it was a tremendous blessing in my life. I can now move on and my heart is filled with peace and hope."

More churches need to spend time researching and identifying that deliverance is real. "Many people deny the existence of Satan and his influence in our lives. Would Christ have used such plain and solemn words repeatedly before His disciples and the Jews to encourage a lying superstition? To deny the reality of demon possession as recorded in the Gospels is simply inconceivable." (*Guide to Spiritual Warfare*, E.M. Bounds, 13.)

In the churches today, the Catholic Church is performing exorcism. The Protestant churches that are Spirit-filled and moving in the fivefold ministry are equipping the saints to do the work of the ministry in deliverance. The Baptist churches that are Spirit-filled and moving in the gifting are also performing deliverance. Calvinist, Lutherans, Assemblies of God, Methodist, Presbyterians, FourSquare Churches and several other denominations that believe are also liberating their people as they are educating them in the process of deliverance. There are several denominations that are not practicing deliverance ministries, who feel that deliverance was in the first century church during Biblical times and they're not venturing to put the Word of God to practice as written in Mark 16:15-18.

The Assembly of God churches are leading along with the Foursquare and the Non-denominational churches in deliverance. The Catholic Church is also working through exorcism to liberate their people as well as the Protestant Church. There are Baptist churches that are Spirit filled that are also coming on board with setting liberty to their captives as well as the Presbyterian Churches who have recently embraced deliverance and are training their members in deliverance. This information is taken from the people who come to us for deliverance and under the International Society of Deliverance Ministers (I.S.D.M.) where lists are provided identifying churches that are participating in setting people free. Deliverance Ministers are contacted and they meet annually so as to have accountability and to discuss new developments that other ministers may be encountering in the field at the local churches.

Chapter Five
Case Scenarios

The following cases are real cases, but the names are changed to protect the individuals. Before we begin discussing the cases, I want to lay down some ground rules for those who will work in deliverance ministry. Establish an environment that is safe for those you will minister to. Fast on the day of the deliverance session. Ensure that you have no doors open to the enemy before you conduct your deliverance session. Bind all the powers that would try to operate during your session in accordance with Matthew 18:18, "Verily, I say unto you, whatsoever ye shall bind on earth shall be bound in heaven: and whatsoever ye shall loose on earth shall be loosed in heaven." Invite the presence of the Holy Spirit to come into the session. Once the Holy Spirit is present, continue to pray in tongues until you begin. Anoint the person with oil to invite the presence of the Holy Spirit to begin His ministry to the individual. If you play music in the background during the deliverance session, keep the music low so as not to interfere with what the Holy Spirit is doing. The music also helps to keep the demons from manifesting during your session. If you don't use music, then continue to pray in tongues for each category of the session.

Real Deliverance Cases of People Who Were Delivered

We will begin to discuss the real case of Tammy Johnson. Tammy was a High Priestess in the kingdom of darkness. Tammy wanted to come out of the kingdom of darkness, but knew if they found out, they would kill her. Tammy had literally moved out of her house and was living in her car when the day her session for deliverance was scheduled. What we did was bring Tammy in and began to minister to her so that she was calm enough to go through the deliverance. Tammy began the session sharing what she had done. Before we could continue in the session of deliverance, we had to lead Tammy to receive Jesus Christ as Lord and Savior. Do not conduct deliverance on anyone who has not received Jesus Christ as Lord and Savior in their life. If you deliver someone who has not received Jesus and their spirit (inner man) house is swept clean, then seven times more demons will return because they did not receive Jesus Christ in their life. Tammy began to share all the evil things she was involved in where innocent children were killed and their blood had been given over to the wizard and warlocks. Tammy had been involved with the occult from when she was a child. She remembers other little children being killed, and she had to watch them die.

Tammy had also taken part in killing other human beings while involved in the occult. When parents are involved in the occult, it is handed down in the generation where the children end up serving and doing just as their parents did.

"The curse affects not only us, but our descendants as well. The curse will continue down the bloodline until it is stopped by repentance and appropriating by faith the redemption provided by Christ through the Cross. The reason curses can perpetuate themselves is that descendants are usually guilty of the same sins as the fathers. When certain sins enter into a family, they open the door for certain spirits to travel from generation to generation. We tend to learn the ways of our ancestors to some degree. It can become a cycle of destruction from generation to generation. Jesus came to stop the cycle of death and destruction. A believer can stop this cycle through repentance and breaking the curse. We can put a stop to the workings of the enemy in our lives, no matter how many generations he has been in operation.

Curses open the door for evil spirits to enter and operate. Again, these evil spirits can operate in families from generation to generation, carrying out their diabolical plan to destroy. One of the keys to deliverance is understanding and breaking curses. (*Identifying and Breaking Curses,* John Eckhardt, 43.)

Tammy had a lot of things that we had to take her through: renunciation of the doors that were opened through her generational lineage. In the occult, Tammy participated in having babies, but when they were born, they were sacrificed to Satan. Although Tammy went through many deep dark things, God was still able to deliver her out of the kingdom of darkness. When

Tammy was delivered, we had to relocate her to another state, and place her under a protection program with a name change so she could live a life serving Jesus Christ.

The next case we will call Larry Houston. Larry was dedicated as a baby to become a warlock in the kingdom of darkness. Larry had dreams of doing bad things from the time he was a child. Larry was dedicated and he belonged to the kingdom of darkness. Larry was dedicated by his father who was a warlock. Larry had no choice as a child of what his future would be when he grew up. When we scheduled an appointment for Larry, we led Larry to Christ. Once Larry received Jesus Christ as Savior, we also took time to take him off the altar of dedication and dedicated him back to Jesus Christ. Larry also had children, and we had to remove all of them off the altar of dedication. Larry's children were having nightmares and could not sleep at night. Larry was led by the Holy Spirit to come to the deliverance ministry. Larry brought his family to seek total deliverance for his entire family. The session was designed to pray over the entire family to liberate them from bondage.

Larry was led through a series of prayers that renounced all the things he had participated in with his father at an early age. He remembers many killings and blood sacrifices of humans and animals. Larry remembers being tied down to the altar and a ceremony taking place when he was seven years old. He could not remember certain things and the Holy Spirit revealed through the seer anointing so we could continue to repent and close the doors to the past. In Larry's life, as well as in his family's life, the deliverance session was successful for Larry and his family.

"Demonic assignment—the strongman is the chief spirit that is assigned to garrison the stronghold. He reinforces the stronghold and ensures the victim's bondage through tight spiritual security. An example of a demonic assignment is the strongman of death, which comes to release the spirit of suicide. Death is the strongman and suicide is the assignment. You can usually know the assignment by the presence of the strongman. Another example is the strongman of Jezebel. By studying the characteristics of Jezebel (such as control, witchcraft, and false prophecy), you can understand the assignment of the spirit. Often, spirits will speak through the mouth of the person and reveal their assignment. A spirit may say, 'I make her see things!' We would be safe to say this was a strongman of divination operating; its assignment was to open up a third eye in her life.

"Point of origination— demons are stupid! Ninety percent of the time they tell on themselves. The only way you find out the true point of origination of a spirit is when it is revealed to you by the Holy Spirit or by one of the demons. I would suggest that anyone make it a habit to conversations with demons. Demons are liars. They have no truth in them, but they can give you pertinent facts to a person's deliverance. The anointing will lock a devil up and make it talk!" (*Clean House Strong House*, Kimberly Daniels, 140.)

Matthew 12:43-45, "When the unclean spirit is gone out of a man, he walketh through dry places, seeking rest, and findeth none. Then he saith, I will return into my house from whence I came out; and when he is come, he findeth it empty, swept, and garnished. Then goeth he, and taketh with himself seven other spirits more wicked than himself, and they enter in and dwell there, and the last state of that man is worse than the first.

"The moment we receive Jesus, every force of darkness that's coming against our life flees. It goes to that desert place looking for a place to rest. Our sin is washed away and the cause of the spiritual curse flees to the desert place. But it comes back later, looking for an open door. Even though our lives have been swept and garnished, blood washed and cleansed, if it finds that we don't understand spiritual curses and we've left a door open, it comes back in and is worse than it was before." (*Free At Last*, Larry Hutch, 61.)

Reasons for Their Captivity

Many people find themselves in captivity because of the sins of the fathers. Generational curses keep families in captivity. When people come to the Kingdom of God and become born-again believers, the next step is for the disciple to take them through deliverance. When they are saved, they are still in their old nature and have a tendency to fall back into their old lifestyle. It is recommended that they go through deliverance while they are training to become converts. When the new believer is delivered, it will ensure that the new converts he or she brings into the Kingdom of God will also go through deliverance. This allows a process to be established for anyone coming into the Kingdom of God.

As ministers, leaders, pastors, and the body of Christ, we have a responsibility to ensure that people are equipped to provide deliverance to those who are in captivity. The reason Tammy was in captivity was because her family raised her in the occult. When we come to the Kingdom of God as a born-again believer, we have a responsibility to close all the doors to the past life we lived in so it will not affect the life God has ordained for us in order to fulfill our destiny.

Tammy had a choice to either stay serving the kingdom of darkness or come out. Tammy chose to come out of captivity and the church was there to help her. When the doors are opened and people want to be set free, we have an obligation to show them how to walk through the door of freedom. Tammy didn't want to continue killing innocent children and other human beings. There are many in the kingdom of darkness who want to come out. Are you prepared to help them?

Larry and his entire family were in captivity because of the generational curse that the father placed on his son as a baby. In many occult situations, parents dedicate the children while they are carried in the womb.

Some of the children don't make it based on the assignment the husband takes for their wives. In Tammy's case, she lost five children when they were born due to sacrifice to the enemy. Tammy played the role of having babies to sacrifice them to the kingdom of darkness. Every time a child was killed, it opened the door to the spirit of murder. When Tammy participated in killing humans, it opened a door that allowed a familiar spirit to travel through Tammy's lineage. Tammy's father allowed that door to be opened for the family. Parents need to be aware of the things they are involved in, which could open doors to their children and grandchildren. Larry's captivity for him and his family was the participation of his father in the occult.

Larry's father was deep in the occult and wanted his son to follow in his footsteps. Larry listened to the voice of the Holy Spirit who had a different future and helped save his family from being in the occult. If we fail to move when God is speaking, we could miss saving a life from total disaster. There are many people who are unaware of the lifestyles their parents lived and many are paying the price. Ignorance is not a way to deny the curses in our lives. We must ask the Holy Spirit to reveal what is in our generational lineage that has not been surfaced so we can close the door to the enemy.

How to Liberate People from Captivity

The first step in liberating people from captivity is that they must acknowledge that they need help. When people are in trouble, they seek the help of the church. When the people come for help, provide them with an application where they can list enough information on what is going on in their lives. The application will have several categories asking about their family history to give the deliverance minister a starting point. Once we receive the application, we review it and pray over it. The Holy Spirit reveals things to us during the review and prayer portion of the application. Once we have completed these steps, schedule an appointment with the individual or family members. At the beginning of the interview, have anointing oil, mints and water available for the individuals and the minister. Having music playing softly provides a relaxing atmosphere where the person can sit and wait in the presence until you are ready; this is highly recommended. When you begin the session, remember to anoint with oil and bind the principalities, powers, and rulers in the area before you begin. Ensure that you as the minister do not have any open doors. If you do, shut those doors before you begin ministering to avoid being attacked during deliverance ministry. When you begin your session, remember to ensure there are no doors to unforgiveness open for the people you are delivering.

If you find that the doors are open, close the doors of unforgiveness first. Check for the doors of bitterness next. Close the access doors. Then you must check to see if there are any doors of resentment with members in their past or present. If you leave the doors open during the session, the Holy Spirit will reveal that the doors are opened and you can go no further until they release the people. If they are not willing to release, it will stop the deliverance session. When you continue, begin to go through the categories on the deliverance application. When you finish, be sure to fill the house with the fruits of the spirits. When you sweep the house, you must put something back in return. If the person has not received the father's or mother's blessing, do ensure that they received the blessing. When you are through with the session and the people leave, make sure that you and your team of two or more are cleansed before you leave. This is to avoid transference of spirits to accompany you home. Be sure you sweep the area where you conducted deliverance so that the place is clean. Physically open the door and command the spirits to leave the building. We find that if you don't cleanse the team after doing deliverance, they have nightmares, and the spirit torments them with the ugly dreams and visions. Do not forget to cleanse your people so they don't take the spirits home to their families. When you have completed liberating people, your next step is to do the actual deliverance.

How to Walk Through Deliverance and Set People Free

While you are in session, some things to look for is if a person is demon possessed, you will sometimes have a foul smell or odor that will signify to you that the demon has come out of them. Remember to command the demons or spirits to leave the person in Jesus' name. You may encounter some stubborn demons then God will reveal to you the name of the strongman. Cut the strongman from the root. Do not go after the branches of the spirits; go after the root. When you pull out the root you have hit a major blow to the kingdom of darkness. If you go after the symptoms, which are the branches of the tree, you are only hitting the surface. You need to go in and press out the deep wounds; take it level by level and bring it up. Remember to allow the person you are delivering breaks between the categories so they can regain their composure.

When you have fully delivered the person, you must make certain that you take time to let them understand the importance of accountability and check in with them after ninety days of the session to see how they are doing. It is recommended that you check in after six months to see if there is a follow-up session needed. If the person has a FreeMasonry background, make sure they pray the prayers of FreeMasonry during the session. This will allow the person to truly be liberated and set free from the generational FreeMasonry. Make sure they go through all the levels even into the Shiners so that you have left no door open. When the session ends, remember to instruct the people to go home and search for objects such as aprons, rings, black books, head garments, or statues of Buddha that may carry a curse, and to destroy them by smashing them and destroying them. If the person was involved in the occult, it is recommended that they get rid of the crystals, crystal balls, mirrors, and all occult objects. If there were occult music, videos, posters, magazines, or drug instruments, we recommend that they are destroyed. A warning: some of the occult objects have demons in them so they need to be burned. To destroy those objects, get a metal trash can and burn them. We destroyed some occult objects where we saw the demons screaming in the fire as they were burning up the objects.

We recommend these steps to avoid the return of the demonic principalities to your home and family. Demons are territorial, so unless you vacate them from the premises, they will remain. It is important that the person who is out of the occult stay connected to the body of Christ during the early stages of their deliverance so as not to fall back into the sin nature they were delivered from.

The next step is called walking it out after the deliverance session. I recommend not doing more than three to six hours in any session. This allows the person as well as the minister and the ministry team to have time to rest.

How to Walk After Deliverance to Maintain Your Freedom

Now this is the most important step of the entire deliverance process for the individual or families you have just conducted deliverance with. The enemy will begin to speak to them right after the session when they leave that they have not been set free. Here is where the person or families must now adopt a new mindset. When we fall into the same sin, it is a familiar pattern that we walked when we were living in iniquity and idolatry. We have to learn how to be transformed by the renewing of the mind. To renew the mind is to think in the opposite light from the kingdom of darkness. Anyone who is delivered must spend time in the Word of God. When reading the Word and praying to the Lord Jesus Christ, you don't have time to commit the sins of the past. The key to shutting the door to the past is to remember that the sin is under the blood, and you have been forgiven for the past sin. Begin to walk as a son and daughter of the living God.

Find a church home. Get involved in a church home group where they can minister to you and your family. If you are a new believer, get involved in the new beginners' class at your local church. When choosing churches for the first time, make certain the church is Spirit filled. Attending Bible study classes will help one grow in the Word. Many people suffer from the spirit of isolation, which is how they fell into the occult to begin with. Instruct the newly delivered to be sure to surround themselves by the body of Christ and not be left alone. The testimony of people who fell right after their deliverance session was due to the fact that they went back to their old patterns and ways of thinking. The deliverance ministers cannot go home with the newly delivered, so they must ensure that they follow the instructions. God is now going to help you if you follow the steps we have provided you.

During the deliverance session, the Holy Spirit will begin to reveal Scriptures to the deliverance ministers and ministry teams on where the person will struggle after the deliverance. The deliverance ministers will need to begin writing those specific Scriptures down during the deliverance session. The Scriptures will help the person receiving deliverance walk out their deliverance successfully.

Chapter Six
Conclusion

I want to encourage pastors and leaders who are ministering in the local churches and in non-profit organizations to keep up the good work. We are making a tremendous change in the lives of God's people. We are seeing whole families restored and property and land taken back. When we continue to help, train, and educate, we find that people can step into the destiny that they have been held back from accomplishing in their lives. We can begin to bring hope to the hopeless. We can train and educate so that other churches are moving and being unified in the things that God has in store for each church. God designed the local church to have the DNA of the Kingdom of Heaven and part of that DNA is Isaiah 61:1-7. We have been anointed to bring glad tidings to the poor to bind up the brokenhearted and to set liberty to the captives.

The question we have to ask pastors and leaders of the local churches or non-profit organizations and deliverance ministries is whether we're doing what God has called us to do. If we are doing what God has called us to do, then why are more people not set free in churches today? What steps are we taking to equip the saints for the work of the ministry? Are we educating and conducting more hands-on training? Are we requiring the teams that we will train up to go through deliverance as well? Are we catching new converts and taking them through deliverance at the beginning before they have been in the church for over twenty years in bondage? Are we sitting around and not focusing on setting people free so they can step into the call to go and make disciples of all nations? When we can say yes to all the questions and the church is moving at 100 percent in making disciples and winning the lost, then we are doing what God has called us to do as the church. The key question is: where do we start? How have we begun to do what God has asked us to do in casting out demons? Are we taking steps to take back what was stolen on land, property, and people?

Works Cited

Balling, Jacob. *The Story Of Christianity From Birth To Global Presence.*
Grand Rapids: William B. Eerdmans, 2003.

Baxter, Mary K., & Lowery, T. L. *A Divine Revelation Of Spiritual Warfare.*
New Kensington: Whitaker House, 2006.

Bounds, E.M. *Guide to Spiritual Warfare.* New Kensington: Publisher
Whitaker House, 2001.

Clark, Randy. *Ministry Training Manual.* Harrisburg: Global Awakening,
2002.

Daniels, Kimberly. *Clean House Strong House.* Charisma House: 2003.

Eckhardt, John. *Deliverance & Spiritual Warfare Manual.* Chicago:
Crusaders Ministries, 1993.

Eckhardt, John. *Identifying & Breaking* Curse. New Kensington: Whitaker
House, 1999.

Elwell, Walter A. *Baker Theological Dictionary Of The Bible.* Grand Rapids:
Baker Books, 1996.

Farwell, Hanna E. *The Sword And The Tambourine, Becoming A Warrior
Through* Worship. Shippensburg: Destiny Image Publishers, Inc.,
2010.

Huch, Larry. *Free At Last, Removing The Past From Your Future*. New Kensington: Whitaker House, 2004.

McGowan, H.B. *The Tabernacle, God's Perfect Plan Of Salvation To All Mankind*. Toronto: World Christian Ministries.

Mears, Henrietta, C, Dr. *What The Bible Is All About Bible Handbook*. Regal Books, 1999.

Martin, Walter, Rische, Martin, Jill, Gorden, Van, Kurt. *The Kingdom Of The Occult*. Nashville: Thomas Nelson, 2008.

Phillips, Ron. *Everyone's Guide To Demons & Spiritual Warfare, Simple, Powerful Tools For Outmaneuvering Satan In Your Daily Life*. Lake Mary: Charisma House, 2010.

Pierce, Chuck D., Systema, Wagner, Rebecca. *Protecting Your Home From Spiritual Darkness*. Ventura: Regal Books, 2004.

Sherman, Dean. *Spiritual Warfare For Every Christian, How To Live In Victory And Retake The Land*. Seattle: Frontline Communications, 1990.

Timmons, J.P. *Mysterious Secrets Of The Dark Kingdom, The Battle For Planet Earth*. Austin: CCI Publishing Company, 1991.

Wagner, Peter C. *Confronting The Queen Of Heaven*. Dallas: Wagner Publications, 2001.

Webster's II. *New Riverside University Dictionary*. Boston: The Riverside Publishing Company, 1994.

Yap, Magrate. *Praise Him With The Tambourine And Dance*. Dallas: Shachah Ministries International, 1990.

About the Author

Reverend Penny Y. Z. Thompson serves as Founder and President of The Greater New Northwest Healing and Deliverance Ministry. The ministry serves in the United States and the nations around the world. Reverend Penny Y.Z. Thompson is currently a retired Army Officer now assigned to serve the Kingdom of God. Reverend Thompson is a graduate of Saint John's University with a BS, a graduate from the Seattle Bible College with a Masters Degree in Renewal Servant Leadership. She is also a graduate from Wagner Leadership Institute.

Reverend Penny has worked in the local ministry for over twenty years and has served in the deliverance ministry for over forty years.

To read more about her travels, media coverage, upcoming schedule of events, and to contact her, please visit her website: http://www. generalsdeliverancemanual.com.

CPSIA information can be obtained at www.ICGtesting.com
Printed in the USA
BVOW010333100212

282636BV00001B/64/P

9 780983 665267